*Repasemos y Continuemos*


**Dr. Charles E. Holloway**

UNIVERSITY OF LOUISIANA AT MONROE

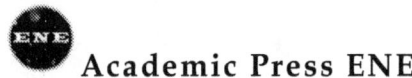
Academic Press ENE

*Repasemos y continuemos*
Dr. Charles E. Holloway
Copyright © 2007
All rights reserved.
No part of this publication may be reproduced, stored in a retrieval system, or transmitted, in any form or by any means (electronic, mechanical, photocopying, recording or otherwise), without the prior written permission of both, the copyright owner and the publisher of this book.
Academic Press ENE
New Jersey, 07704, USA
http://www.editorial-ene.com/index2.htm
AcademicPressENE@aol.com
Second Edition, September, 2007
ISBN: 1-930879-51-2

# CONTENTS

| | |
|---|---|
| Introduction........................................................................................................... | 7 |
| Chapter 1: The Indicative Tenses........................................................................ | 11 |
| Chapter 2: Nouns and Articles............................................................................. | 35 |
| Chapter 3: Pronouns............................................................................................. | 53 |
| Chapter 4: Preterit and Imperfect....................................................................... | 73 |
| Chapter 5: Ser and Estar...................................................................................... | 89 |
| Chapter 6: Adjectives........................................................................................... | 101 |
| Chapter 7: The Subjunctive in Noun Clauses................................................... | 113 |
| Chapter 8: The Subjunctive in Adjective and Adverbial Clauses.................. | 129 |
| Chapter 9: Other Uses of the Subjunctive and Commands............................ | 137 |
| Chapter 10: Adverbs, Prepositions, and Conjunctions.................................... | 147 |
| Chapter 11: Nonfinites and Reverse Constructions........................................ | 163 |
| Appendix I: Verb Conjugations.......................................................................... | 173 |
| Appendix II: Verb List......................................................................................... | 187 |
| References............................................................................................................. | 199 |
| Index...................................................................................................................... | 201 |

# Introduction

The title of this book, *Repasemos y Continuemos*, is very much indicative of its intended purpose. It is designed for students who have already been introduced to the fundamentals of Spanish grammar and wish to enhance their knowledge and reach the next level of understanding. Throughout the book, the goal is to take intermediate students back to a point in their understanding of Spanish grammar where they feel comfortable and proceed to a point well beyond where they began. By moving from the known to the unknown, students gain a broader and deeper understanding of the material presented without feeling overwhelmed or threatened by the process.

The purpose of this book is very narrow. It is designed to enhance the intermediate student's understanding of Spanish grammar by providing an opportunity to analyze and discuss grammar in a more detailed way than is generally possible in classes which emphasize mastery of all four skills. It is intended to supplement other materials, methods, and activities used in the classroom. It is designed to build oral proficiency only indirectly by improving grammatical competence. Its target audience is post-secondary Spanish students who are involved in a well-rounded language program that provides diverse opportunities for hearing, reading, writing, and speaking the language. In short, this book is intended to be used as one element of a multi-faceted approach to language learning.

Given that this book is intended to help students enhance their knowledge of Spanish grammar, it may be helpful to investigate very briefly what is meant by the term grammar, and exactly how and why one should study it. For many people the word grammar may conjure up visions of elementary or high school classes where they were taught the evils of splitting infinitives or ending a sentence with a preposition. Used in this way, the word grammar involves knowing the "dos" and "don'ts" of "correct" usage. Native speakers of a language must be instructed about what is right and what is wrong with regard to its "correct" usage. This idea of grammar as an explicit set of rules which must be adhered to is sometimes referred to as the *prescriptive approach* to language.

The prescriptive approach to language can be contrasted with the *descriptive approach* in which the language is viewed dispassionately without value judgments about what is correct and what is incorrect. Most linguists subscribe to a more descriptive approach to language. They describe and make observations about a language as it is actually used by its speakers without attempting to enforce rules which prescribe how it "should" be spoken.

The idea that a fully fluent native speaker might need to be told how to speak his or her language brings up yet another definition of grammar. The knowledge every competent native speaker has about his or her native language, including syntax, semantics, phonology, and pragmatics, is sometimes referred to as a *mental grammar*. The mental grammar of a native speaker may, and very often does, differ from the prescriptive model of the language. It is this mental grammar that linguists seek to describe.

Actually, prescriptivism and descriptivism are not clearly defined or discrete categories; they are more like endpoints on a continuum. If all those individuals who are currently engaged in the study or the teaching of languages were asked to assess themselves with regard to their own views about prescriptivism and descriptivism, there would likely be marks at every point on the continuum. Some view prescriptivism as an elitist form of linguistic snobbery. Others maintain that there is a need for rules that govern "correct" usage. C. Edward Good (2002: 419) makes the point this way: "Words matter. The way they come together to convey meaning is governed by a set of rules. Either you know it or you don't ."

Given the considerable degree of linguistic variation found among the many Spanish dialects throughout the world, one might wonder if it is even possible to make reference to a "standard" Spanish language. Actually, this question may be somewhat easier to answer with regard to Spanish than would be the case for English. This is attributible in large measure to the existence of the Real Academia Española which was established in 1713 in order to preserve and continue the Spanish language. Although the RAE is often criticized as being too conservative, its considerable influence may improve the prospects for maintenance of a standard written language (see Pountain 2003: 265-267).

Regardless of how one feels about whether or not a native speaker should be told how to speak his or her first language, the issue of "correctness" becomes somewhat more focused when discussing second language learners. In this case, the major goal is for learners to speak, read, write, and understand the language as native speakers do. As anyone who has studied a second language knows, this is a high standard which many fail to achieve.

Grammatical mistakes are an inevitable part of the language-learning process. But should these errors be viewed or treated in the same way as prescriptive errors made in one's native language? The difference, of course, is that the mistakes second language learners make are often very different from those made by native speakers. Errors made by non-native speakers which are at odds with the mental grammars and common usage of native speakers would not be viewed as acceptable even from a descriptivist point of view.

But how important is it to correct second language errors? After all, most practitioners and researchers in the field of second language acquisition today believe that errors are a natural part of the learning process. Many researchers believe that second language learners construct their own internal representation of the target language. This language system, most often referred to as *interlanguage*, is similar to and different from both the native and target language. It is believed that this system gradually becomes less like the learner's native language and more like the target language throughout the language-learning process.

While there is some disagreement about the exact nature of interlanguage and about how it is changed, most second language researchers agree that errors are a normal and inevitable part of the language-learning process. However, this somewhat liberating idea that errors are to be expected does not negate the fact that there are some concerns associated with not paying attention to mistakes made by second language learners. Many of those conducting research in the field of second language acquisition believe that in the absence of corrective feedback second language learners may retain some non-native elements of their developing interlanguage systems. This retention of incorrect linguistic forms is often referred to as *fossilization*.

Many practitioners in the field of second language acquisition believe that corrective feedback, particularly in a form that is viewed by the learner as constructive and positive, represents one way to minimize fossilization. But is error correction really necessary? So long as the language learner gets his or her point across, is there really any justification for being so concerned about the errors he or she makes in the target language?

In fact, there is some evidence to suggest that, depending on the target culture and the type of error involved, some native speakers do react negatively to learner errors (Chastain 1980, Ensz 1982, Piazza 1980, Ludwig 1984). Native speaker reactions indicate that errors made by non-native speakers can range from those that native speakers find mildly irritating to some that would be considered downright stigmatizing. So, it would appear that there are sound reasons for giving at least some attention to grammatical accuracy.

Many researchers in the field of second language acquisition have advocated the use of careful-style grammar exercises in which conscious attention is given to the forms of the language (Tarone 1983, Ellis 1985, Lightblown 1990). While few language teachers would advocate a return to second language "methodology" that emphasizes endless rules and rote drills *to the exclusion of everything else*, many still believe that grammatical instruction and form-focused practice can be a very beneficial component of the language teacher's repertoire of techniques, activities, and assessment tools. Careful-style activities should be used in conjunction with a variety of other activities representing all points on the careful style/vernacular style continuum. Activities in this book, which would be located very much at the careful style end of the continuum, are meant to complement other language-learning activities that are located at many different points.

The explicit teaching of grammar also serves another very important function. The fact is that some of those who take language courses will themselves end up being language teachers. Whether or not one feels that having an understanding of the rules of grammar is helpful to beginning students, most would agree that those who plan to teach should have a more thorough understanding of how the language works. Highlighting the difficulties faced by teachers who themselves lack such metalinguistic knowledge, Debra Myhill (2000: 162) makes the following point: "As a consequence they are unable to help pupils at precisely where learning becomes difficult. Like spelling, grammar is easier to correct than teach, because correction relies on implicit knowledge, whilst teaching demands explicit knowledge."

The following chapters contain prescriptive grammar rules and suggestions for "correct" usage. However, this book represents but one of the many tools required in order to build linguistic competence. Those using this information should be ever mindful of the fact that Spanish is a living and evolving language that is used by real people who have their own ideas about how the language is spoken or should be spoken. With this in mind, students should maintain a clear focus on the ultimate goal of language study: being able to communicate appropriately and effectively in the target language.

The publication of this book would be incomplete without the acknowledgment of several individuals whose help and support were invaluable during the process of its creation and revision. First and foremost, I would like to express appreciation to my family, in particular to my wife, Carol, and to her mother, Barbara, who always offer encouragement and support for any project I choose to undertake. I would also like to thank my friend and former student, Joshua Legg, for his meticulous examination of the first edition of this text. His comments and suggestions were most helpful to me in completing the revised edition. Finally, I would like to acknowledge my current and former colleagues and students at the University of Louisiana at Monroe for contributing on a daily basis to my ongoing process of learning and discovery.

# CHAPTER 1

# The Indicative Tenses

## Present Indicative

**Regular Verb Conjugations**

The Spanish infinitive consists of a stem and an ending. The infinitive **comer**, for example, has a stem **com-** and an ending **-er**. The three types of regular verbs are classified according to their endings as **-ar**, **-er**, and **-ir**. Regular verbs, which do not show any changes in their stems, are conjugated by adding the conjugation endings for each type of verb to the stem of the verb. There are three sets of conjugation endings for regular verbs. The endings for **-ar** verbs in the present indicative are **-o, -as, -a, -amos, -áis,** and **-an**. The endings for **-er** verbs are **-o, -es, -e, -emos, -éis,** and **-en**. For **-ir** verbs the endings are **-o, -es, -e, -imos, -ís,** and **-en**. The **nosotros** and **vosotros** forms are stressed on the vowel in the verb ending, while the other forms are stressed on a vowel in the stem.

| **Present Tense Conjugations: Regular Verbs** | | | | |
|---|---|---|---|---|
| **Person** | Subject Pronoun | -AR | -ER | IR |
| | | Hablar | Comer | Vivir |
| **Singular** | | | | |
| 1st | yo | hablo | como | vivo |
| 2nd | tú | hablas | comes | vives |
| 3rd | él, ella usted | habla | come | vive |
| **Plural** | | | | |
| 1st | nosotros (as) | hablamos | comemos | vivimos |
| 2nd | vosotros (as) | habláis | coméis | vivís |
| 3rd | ellos, ellas ustedes | hablan | comen | viven |

## Spelling-Change Verbs

A change in the spelling of some verbs is required so that they will reflect the actual pronunciation. Because these changes are predictable in Spanish, they are not regarded as "irregular" by most teachers or grammarians. In some cases these changes can be attributed to the evolution from Latin to Spanish since some Spanish consonants came to have more than one sound depending upon which vowels they preceded. In other cases, a verb form must carry a written accent in order to make the orthographic form agree with its pronunciation. These orthographic changes are noted in the chart below.

### Present Tense Conjugations: Spelling-Change Verbs

| c to zc (-cer, -cir) | gu to g (-guir) | c to z (-cer) | g to j (-ger, -gir) |
|---|---|---|---|
| **Conocer** | **Distinguir** | **Convencer** | **Coger** |
| conozco | distingo | convenzo | cojo |
| conoces | distingues | convences | coges |
| conoce | distingue | convence | coge |
| conocemos | distinguimos | convencemos | cogemos |
| conocéis | distinguís | convencéis | cogéis |
| conocen | distinguen | convencen | cogen |
| | | | |
| Other **c to zc** verbs: | Other **gu to g** verbs: | Other **c to z** verbs: | Other **g to j** verbs: |
| traducir | extinguir | vencer | escoger |
| conducir | | ejercer | proteger |
| parecer | | | corregir |
| merecer | | | dirigir |
| obedecer | | | exigir |
| ofrecer | | | |

| i to í (-iar) | u to ú (-uar) | i to y (-uir) |
|---|---|---|
| **Enviar** | **Actuar** | **Incluir** |
| envío | actúo | incluyo |
| envías | actúas | incluyes |
| envía | actúa | incluye |
| enviamos | actuamos | incluimos |
| enviáis | actuáis | incluís |
| envían | actúan | incluyen |
| | | |
| Other **i to í** verbs: | Other **u to ú** verbs: | Other **i to y** verbs: |
| confiar | continuar | construir |
| criar | graduar | contribuir |
| guiar | | destruir |
| | | huir |

## Irregular Verb Conjugations

### Stem-Changing Verbs

Many verbs which have a stressed **é** or **ó** as the last vowel of the stem have a stem change of **e to ie, o to ue**, or **e** to **i**. The stem changes for **-ar** and **-er** verbs are **e** to **ie** or **o** to **ue**. A few **-ir** verbs have the change of **e to i**. Because the stressed syllable of the **nosotros** and **vosotros** forms is not in the stem, these do not have a stem change. Although most authors classify stem-changing verbs as "irregular," Stanley Whitley (1986: 86-91) makes a very persuasive argument for the predictability and regularity of these changes.

---

**Present Tense Conjugations: Stem-Changing Verbs**

| e to ie | o to ue | e to i |
|---|---|---|
| **Pensar** | **Dormir** | **Pedir** |
| pienso | duermo | pido |
| piensas | duermes | pides |
| piensa | duerme | pide |
| pensamos | dormimos | pedimos |
| pensáis | dormís | pedís |
| piensan | duermen | piden |
| | | |
| Other **e to ie** verbs: | Other **o to ue** verbs: | Other **e to i** verbs: |
| cerrar | acostarse | conseguir |
| comenzar | costar | despedir |
| convertir | devolver | reír |
| empezar | encontrar | repetir |
| encender | llover | servir |
| entender | morir | vestirse |
| defender | mover | |
| divertirse | poder | |
| querer | probar | |
| perder | recordar | |
| preferir | | |
| mentir | | |
| sugerir | | |

## Verbs with an Irregular First-Person Singular Form

Some verbs have an irregularity only in the **yo** form. It will be necessary for students to memorize the irregular first-person forms of these verbs.

---

**Present Tense Conjugations: Irregular First-Person Singular Verbs**

| Hacer | Poner | Salir | Traer | Caer | Valer |
|---|---|---|---|---|---|
| hago | pongo | salgo | traigo | caigo | valgo |
| haces | pones | sales | traes | caes | vales |
| hace | pone | sale | trae | cae | vale |
| hacemos | ponemos | salimos | traemos | caemos | valemos |
| hacéis | ponéis | salís | traéis | caéis | valéis |
| hacen | ponen | salen | traen | caen | valen |

| Dar | Saber | Ver | Caber |
|---|---|---|---|
| doy | sé | veo | quepo |
| das | sabes | ves | cabes |
| da | sabe | ve | cabe |
| damos | sabemos | vemos | cabemos |
| dais | sabéis | veis | cabéis |
| dan | saben | ven | caben |

---

## Stem-Change and Irregular First-Person Singular Verbs

A few verbs have a stem change as well as an irregular first person spelling change. As was the case for the stem-changing verbs above, the first-person plural and second-person plural forms do not have a stem change.

---

**Present Tense Conjugations: Verbs with an Irregular Yo Form and a Stem Change**

| Tener | Venir | Decir | Seguir | Conseguir |
|---|---|---|---|---|
| tengo | vengo | digo | sigo | consigo |
| tienes | vienes | dices | sigues | consigues |
| tiene | viene | dice | sigue | consigue |
| tenemos | venimos | decimos | seguimos | conseguimos |
| tenéis | venís | decís | seguís | conseguís |
| tienen | vienen | dicen | siguen | consiguen |

**Other Irregular Present Tense Verbs**

Some verbs in the present tense are irregular and must be memorized. As the chart below indicates, some of the verbs with the greatest irregularities in the present tense are among the most common verbs in the language.

| Present Tense Conjugations: Irregular Verbs | | | |
|---|---|---|---|
| **Ir** | **Ser** | **Estar** | **Oír** |
| voy | soy | estoy | oigo |
| vas | eres | estás | oyes |
| va | es | está | oye |
| vamos | somos | estamos | oímos |
| vais | sois | estáis | oís |
| van | son | están | oyen |

## Use of the Present Indicative

In terms of order, the present tense is simultaneous with the event of speaking. In both Spanish and English, the present tense is used to state what is true in the present or what is universally true (Iglesias and Meiden 1995: 169). The present tense is most often used in English to indicate habitual actions that are not going on at the moment of speaking.

| | |
|---|---|
| Yo hablo francés. | *I speak French.* |
| Ellos trabajan mucho. | *They work a lot.* |

However, as Solé and Solé (1977: 1) note, the present tense may also be used in Spanish to describe events in progress at the moment of speaking, repeated actions, ongoing states, intended actions, or future actions.

| | | |
|---|---|---|
| Juan habla por teléfono ahora. | *Juan is talking on the phone now.* | (progressive) |
| Ellos comen tacos todos los días. | *They eat tacos every day.* | (repeated) |
| Ella está enferma. | *She is sick.* | (present state) |
| Voy al cine esta noche. | *I am going to the movies tonight.* | (future) |

The use of the present tense is more limited in English; it is not generally used with most verbs to describe ongoing action in the present. The present tense is not used in English to express a future perspective unless it is accompanied by an adverbial expression which denotes futurity: *I leave tomorrow*. As noted above, Spanish does often use the simple present to describe an event that is in progress. The parallel English constructions usually describe habitual actions. English requires the progressive to show events in progress.

| | |
|---|---|
| *She studies Spanish.* | (habitual) |
| *She is studying Spanish.* | (in progress) |

**Exercise 1.** Conjugate the verbs in parentheses in the present indicative tense.

1. ellos (to destroy) _____
2. nosotros (to buy) _____
3. yo (to protect) _____
4. ustedes (to arrive) _____
5. tú (to travel) _____
6. usted (to believe) _____
7. Juan (to receive) _____
8. yo (to graduate) _____
9. él (to run) _____
10. nosotros (to watch) _____
11. ellos (to build) _____
12. tú (to send) _____
13. yo (to overcome) _____
14. usted (to distinguish) _____
15. ella (to deserve) _____
16. ustedes (to look for) _____
17. María y Elena (to see) _____
18. ella (to seem) _____
19. yo (to correct) _____
20. ellos (to act) _____
21. nosotros (to demand) _____
22. yo (to obey) _____
23. usted (to try) _____
24. tú (to sell) _____
25. ella (to remain) _____
26. él (to guide) _____
27. mis tíos (to choose) _____
28. yo (to contribute) _____

**Exercise 2.** Translate the following sentences to Spanish.

1. I know the girl who drives that car.
_____

2. They are taking the toys to the children.
_____

3. We demand that they stay here.
_____

4. Her friends treat her badly, but she doesn't deserve it.
_____

5. I am directing the committee that is planning the trip.
_____

6. He always laughs when he remembers that story.
_____

7. I don't confide in my parents because they don't understand me.
_____

8. The students always leave us when they graduate.
_____

9. Ana always guides me when I have to choose a class.
_____

10. Her boyfriend seems to be a very inquisitive person.
_____

**Exercise 3.** Conjugate the following verbs in the present indicative tense.

1. ellos (to see) _____
2. ustedes (to follow) _____
3. mis papás (to go) _____
4. yo (to hear) _____
5. ella (to do) _____
6. nosotros (to find) _____
7. tú (to turn on) _____
8. yo (to laugh) _____
9. ella (to sleep) _____
10. él (to go) _____
11. nosotros (to say, tell) _____
12. ellos (to play) _____
13. ustedes (to suggest) _____
14. tú (to flee) _____
15. él (to continue) _____
16. yo (to thank) _____
17. ella (to taste) _____
18. ellos (to order, ask for) _____
19. ustedes (to put, place) _____
20. yo (to fall) _____
21. Juan (to repeat) _____
22. mi novia (to bring) _____
23. yo (to choose) _____
24. yo (to lose) _____
25. ustedes (to lie) _____
26. tú (to get dressed) _____
27. mi maleta (to fit) _____
28. yo (to obey) _____

**Exercise 4.** Translate the following sentences to Spanish.

1. My friends always have a good time at my parties.
_____

2. Marcos always tells the truth, but his friends lie.
_____

3. We are lucky, but we always lose money when we go to Las Vegas.

_____

4. They never order chicken when they come to this restaurant.

_____

5. I want to eat because I am dying of hunger.

_____

6. My wife is afraid because I am driving.

_____

7. I always put the food on the table for them.

_____

8. Do you know where your children are?

_____

9. I translate the documents, and she corrects them.

_____

10. If you want to get good grades, you have to work more.

_____

# Present Progressive

The present progressive is formed by combining the present tense of the verb **estar** with the present participle form. The present participle is formed by removing the **-ar, -er,** and **-ir** endings from the infinitive and adding **-ando** for **-ar** verbs and **-iendo** for **-er** and **-ir** verbs. **-Ir** verbs that have a stem change in the third-person forms of the preterit tense will have the same change in the present participle. Irregular present participle forms include **leyendo, durmiendo, pidiendo, sirviendo, creyendo,** and **diciendo.** The present progressive is rarely used with verbs of being and verbs of motion such as **ser, estar, ir,** and **venir.**

| Present Progressive Tense Conjugations: Regular Verbs | | |
|---|---|---|
| **Hablar** | **Comer** | **Vivir** |
| estoy hablando | estoy comiendo | estoy viviendo |
| estás hablando | estás comiendo | estás viviendo |
| está hablando | está comiendo | está viviendo |
| estamos hablando | estamos comiendo | estamos viviendo |
| estáis hablando | estáis comiendo | estáis viviendo |
| están hablando | están comiendo | están viviendo |

As was previously noted in this chapter, Spanish very often uses the simple present tense to express ongoing action while English does so infrequently. However, both English and Spanish may require that the present tense be used for some actions that are in progress at the moment of speaking. For example, speakers of both languages would use the simple present tense rather than the present progressive for ongoing emotional states such as *love* or *hate*.

*Estoy odiándolos.          *I am hating them.
*Ellos están amando a sus hijos.       *They are loving their children.

English sometimes uses the present progressive to speak of planned actions. In Spanish the simple present, periphrastic future, or the future tense are used to express this idea. English speakers must avoid using the present progressive in Spanish to express future intent. Because the simple present tense is used more often than the present progressive in Spanish, even for ongoing actions, English speakers would be well advised to avoid overusing the present progressive.

*Está estudiando español conmigo mañana.      (incorrect)
She is studying Spanish with me tomorrow.       (future)

Estudia con ellos esta noche.
She is studying with them tonight.               (future)

Va a estudiar esta noche.
She is going to study tonight.                    (future)

**Exercise 5.** Conjugate the following in the present progressive tense.

1. yo (to read) _____         2. ellos (to speak) _____

3. usted (to sleep) _____       4. él (to serve) _____

5. ella (to bring) _____        6. tú (to eat) _____

7. ustedes (to do, make) _____    8. él (to breathe) _____

9. Juan (to look for) _____       10. nosotros (to buy) _____

11. mis hijos (to ask for, order) _____    12. Ana y Marcos (to say, tell) _____

# Imperfect Progressive

| Imperfect Progressive Tense Conjugations: Regular Verbs | | |
|---|---|---|
| **Hablar** | **Comer** | **Vivir** |
| estaba hablando | estaba comiendo | estaba viviendo |
| estabas hablando | estabas comiendo | estabas viviendo |
| estaba hablando | estaba comiendo | estaba viviendo |
| estábamos hablando | estábamos comiendo | estábamos viviendo |
| estabais hablando | estabais comiendo | estabais viviendo |
| estaban hablando | estaban comiendo | estaban viviendo |

The imperfect progressive is formed by using the imperfect tense of the verb **estar** and the present participle. It is used to show that an action was in the process of happening at some point in the past. Both the imperfect progressive and the imperfect tense are used to show continuous or ongoing action in the past.

Yo estaba comiendo cuando ella llegó.  *I was eating when she arrived.*
Mientras miraba la televisión me llamó.  *While I was watching TV he called me.*

**Exercise 6.** Conjugate the following verbs in the imperfect progressive tense.

| | |
|---|---|
| 1. ella (to laugh) _____ | 2. mi mamá (to give) _____ |
| 3. el hombre (to lie) _____ | 4. tus amigos (to play) _____ |
| 5. yo (to put, place) _____ | 6. ustedes (to count) _____ |
| 7. tú (to cry) _____ | 8. mi amiga (to ski) _____ |
| 9. sus hermanos (to sing) _____ | 10. la familia (to watch, look at) _____ |

**Exercise 7.** Translate the following sentences to Spanish.

1. We are going to send the passengers their tickets.

_____

2. My brother always gets dressed without looking at a mirror.

_____

3. I demand that you return the package to me.

_____

4. I am going to the store. I'll be back at six.

_____

5. Ricardo suggests that we leave the building.

_____

6. Her sister was playing soccer when she broke her arm.

_____

7. My sister-in-law is leaving for Florida on Friday.

_____

8. You (plural) should be careful; you are going to get burned.

_____

9. While I was talking to my lawyer, the policeman entered the room.

_____

10. She is coming to our house.

_____

## Present Perfect

| Present Perfect Tense Conjugations: Regular Verbs | | |
|---|---|---|
| **Hablar** | **Comer** | **Vivir** |
| he hablado | he comido | he vivido |
| has hablado | has comido | has vivido |
| ha hablado | ha comido | ha vivido |
| hemos hablado | hemos comido | hemos vivido |
| habéis hablado | habéis comido | habéis vivido |
| han hablado | han comido | han vivido |

The present perfect tense is formed by combining the present tense of the verb **haber** and the past participle form. The regular past participle is formed by removing the **-ar** ending from the infinitive and adding **-ado** for **-ar** verbs and **-ido** for **-er** and **-ir** verbs. When used as part of the perfect tense, the past participle forms will always end in **-o**. **-Er** verbs whose stems end in a vowel will have an accent mark over the **-i-** in the past participle froms. Thus, **creer** and **leer** have past participle forms of **creído** and **leído**, respectively. Some common irregular past participle forms are shown below.

| Irregular Past Participle Forms | | | |
|---|---|---|---|
| abrir | **abierto** | poner | **puesto** |
| cubrir | **cubierto** | romper | **roto** |
| decir | **dicho** | ver | **visto** |
| hacer | **hecho** | volver | **vuelto** |
| escribir | **escrito** | devolver | **devuelto** |
| morir | **muerto** | envolver | **envuelto** |

No other word may come between the verb **haber** and the past participle form in Spanish. The adverb **no** and the object pronouns must precede the verb. Other adverbial expressions such as **todavía** and **ya** may precede or follow the past participle form.

| | |
|---|---|
| Yo le he mandado la carta. | *I have sent him the letter.* |
| Juan no se ha bañado. | *Juan has not bathed.* |

The present perfect describes an action which was completed before the present, but has some relevance to what is happening in the present. Whether or not one uses the present perfect depends upon how relevant to the present time the action or event is considered to be.

| | |
|---|---|
| Ellos han comido los tacos. | *They have eaten the tacos.* |
| No hemos dicho la verdad. | *We have not told the truth.* |
| ¿Has visto la película? | *Have you seen the movie?* |

In both Spanish and English, the present perfect tense is used to relate a past event to the present. For this reason, the present perfect is often used with adverbial expressions such as **hoy, este mes,** or **este siglo** which would be considered within the time frame of grammatical present.

| | |
|---|---|
| Hoy no la he visto ni una sola vez. | *I have not seen her a single time today.* |
| Esta semana la he visto varias. | *This week I have seen her several times.* |

When present perfect occurs without any modifiers, it describes a completed event which is viewed as relevant to what is happening in the present time.

| | |
|---|---|
| Ha estado muy enferma. | *She has been very sick (and may still be).* |
| Estuvo muy enferma. | *She was very sick.* |
| Ha sido un estudiante trabajador. | *He has been a hardworking student.* |
| Fue un estudiante trabajador. | *He was a hardworking student (something changed).* |

While it is the preterit tense which is most often used with adverbials that do not include grammatical present such as **ayer, el mes pasado,** and **el año pasado,** the present perfect may also be used in Spanish to refer to a specific point in the past. It should be noted that this usage is not universal throughout the Spanish-speaking world. As illustrated by the following examples from Solé and Solé (1977: 17), in English the present perfect is only used in relation to indefinite past reference; the simple past is used for definite or specific past reference.

| | |
|---|---|
| Su hija se ha casado el año pasado. | *His daughter got married last year.* |
| Ayer ha trabajado todo el día. | *Yesterday she worked all day.* |

As John Butt and Carmen Benjamin (1988: 209) point out, Spanish uses the present perfect wherever English does, but the Spanish present perfect must often be translated by the simple past in English. Thus, if the present perfect is used as it would be in English, mistakes are unlikely.

**Exercise 8.** Conjugate the following verbs in the present perfect tense.

1. ella (to put, place) _____

2. nosotros (to see) _____

3. ellos (to say, tell) _____

4. mi tío (to die) _____

5. nuestros amigos (to go) _____

6. Marisol (to break) _____

7. yo (to do, make) _____

8. tú (to come) _____

9. la tienda (to close) _____

10. todo el mundo (to leave) _____

11. usted (to write) _____

12. yo (to eat) _____

13. mi mamá (to receive) _____

14. ellos (to lose) _____

## Past Perfect (or Pluperfect)

The past perfect tense is formed by using the imperfect tense of **haber** and the past participle. This tense is used to describe an action that took place further back in time than another past action which is usually expressed in the preterit or imperfect tense.

| Past Perfect Tense Conjugations: Regular Verbs | | |
|---|---|---|
| **Hablar** | **Comer** | **Vivir** |
| había hablado | había comido | había vivido |
| habías hablado | habías comido | habías vivido |
| había hablado | había comido | había vivido |
| habíamos hablado | habíamos comido | habíamos vivido |
| habíais hablado | habíais comido | habíais vivido |
| habían hablado | habían comido | habían vivido |

| | |
|---|---|
| Ya había comido cuando ella llegó. | *I had already eaten when she arrived.* |
| Quería verlos, pero ya habían salido. | *She wanted to see them, but they had already left.* |

**Exercise 9.** Conjugate the following verbs in the past perfect indicative.

1. ella (to cover)_____
2. ustedes (to play) _____
3. tu hermana (to order, ask for) _____
4. ellos (to move) _____
5. nosotros (to take) _____
6. nuestra abuela (to call) _____
7. los empleados (to send) _____
8. yo (to take out) _____
9. tú (to drink) _____
10. mis amigos (to clean) _____

# Future

| Future Tense Conjugations: Regular Verbs | | |
|---|---|---|
| **Hablar** | **Comer** | **Vivir** |
| hablaré | comeré | viviré |
| hablarás | comerás | vivirás |
| hablará | comerá | vivirá |
| hablaremos | comeremos | viviremos |
| hablaréis | comeréis | viviréis |
| hablarán | comerán | vivirán |

The future tense is formed by adding the conjugation endings **-é, -ás, á, -emos, -éis**, and **án** to the infinitive. Because the entire infinitive form is used, there is only one set of endings for this tense. There are several common irregular stems for the future tense.

| Irregular Future Tense Stems | | | |
|---|---|---|---|
| caber | cabr- | querer | querr- |
| decir | dir- | saber | sabr- |
| haber | habr- | salir | saldr- |
| hacer | har- | tener | tendr- |
| poder | podr- | valer | valdr- |
| poner | pondr- | venir | vendr- |

The future tense describes an event which is subsequent to the moment of speaking. It is less commonly used in informal contexts than either the periphrastic **ir a + infinitive** construction or the present tense with adverbial expressions denoting future such as **mañana**, **el mes que viene**, **esta tarde**, etc.

| | |
|---|---|
| Comeremos con ellos esta noche. | *We will eat with them tonight* |
| Pondré la comida en la mesa. | *I will put the food on the table.* |
| Te dirá cuando lleguen. | *He will tell you when they arrive.* |

In some cases the future tense may be distinguished from the other two ways of expressing the future by the speaker's intended degree of certainty. Although the distinction is often a subtle one, use of the future tense may indicate a lesser degree of certainty. The future tense seems to be losing ground in everyday speech as a way to talk about future actions (see Butt & Benjamin 1988: 203).

Iremos al teatro esta noche.                         (less certain)
*We're going to go to the theater tonight.*

Vamos al teatro esta noche.                          (more definite)
*We are going to the theater tonight.*

Hablaremos con ellos.                                (less certain)
*Let's talk with them.*

Vamos a hablar con ellos.                            (more definite)
*We are going to talk with them.*

Because the future tense is used to refer to events that have not yet occurred, it is sometimes used to express probability. This usage is sometimes referred to as the *future of probability* or the *suppositional future*. When used in this way, the future tense is often translated in English with the present tense and "must" or "probably."

Alguien toca la puerta. Será Juan.        *Someone is knocking on the door. It must be Juan.*

Ana no está aquí. Estará enferma.         *Ana is not here. She is probably sick.*

**Exercise 10.** Conjugate the following verbs in the future tense.

1. ella (to put, place) _____     2. tu mamá (to cook) _____

3. mis primos (to do, make) _____     4. yo (to leave) _____

5. ustedes (to change) _____     6. tú (to say, tell) _____

7. nosotros (to have) _____     8. usted (to arrive) _____

9. Ana y Marta (to come) _____     10. él (can, to be able to) _____

11. ella (to return) _____     12. nuestro papá (to give) _____

13. yo (to stay) _____     14. ella (to buy) _____

## Future Perfect

| **Future Perfect Tense Conjugations: Regular Verbs** | | |
|---|---|---|
| **Hablar** | **Comer** | **Vivir** |
| habré hablado | habré comido | habré vivido |
| habrás hablado | habrás comido | habrás vivido |
| habrá hablado | habrá comido | habrá vivido |
| habremos hablado | habremos comido | habremos vivido |
| habréis hablado | habréis comido | habréis vivido |
| habrán hablado | habrán comido | habrán vivido |

The future perfect tense is formed by combining the future tense of **haber** and the past participle. With the future perfect tense, the speaker anticipates that an event will have been completed by a certain point. Like the future tense, the future perfect may also be used to express probability or conjecture. In such cases, the future perfect tense in often translated in English as *have (or has) probably + past participle*.

| | |
|---|---|
| Habremos comido para las seis. | *We will have eaten by six.* |
| Habrán vuelto para el lunes. | *They will have returned by Monday.* |
| Habremos terminado cuando llegues. | *We will have finished when you arrive.* |
| No tiene hambre; habrá comido. | *She is not hungry. She has probably eaten.* |

**Exercise 11.** Conjugate the following verbs in the future perfect indicative.

1. ella (to leave) _____

2. ustedes (to finish) _____

3. mi esposa (to give) _____

4. mis hermanos (to see) _____

5. todos (to sell) _____

6. yo (to turn on) _____

7. ella (to wash) _____

8. tú (to go to bed) _____

9. nosotros (to win) _____

10. tu familia (to have) _____

## Conditional

The conditional tense is formed by adding the conjugation endings **-ía, -ías, -ía, -íamos,** and **-ían** to the infinitive. As was the case with the future tense, there is only one set of endings for all three verb types. The irregular stems for the conditional are the same as those for the future tense. The conditional describes an event as happening subsequent to another past action. For this reason, the conditional is often used in indirect discourse.

| Conditional Tense Conjugations: Regular Verbs | | |
|---|---|---|
| **Hablar** | **Comer** | **Vivir** |
| hablaría | comería | viviría |
| hablarías | comerías | vivirías |
| hablaría | comería | viviría |
| hablaríamos | comeríamos | viviríamos |
| hablaríais | comeríais | viviríais |
| hablarían | comerían | vivirían |

Ellos irán mañana.  (direct discourse)
*They will go tomorrow.*

Los estudiantes harán la tarea.  (direct discourse)
*The students will do the homework.*

Dijeron que irían mañana.  (indirect discourse)
*They said that they would go tomorrow.*

Dijeron que harían la tarea.  (indirect discourse)
*They said that they would do the homework.*

As was the case with the future and future perfect tenses, the conditional may be used to express probability. Because the conditional is a past tense, the expression of probability is from a past perspective. This is equivalent in many cases to the English use of *probably* with the past tense.

Alguien tocó la puerta.  *Someone knocked on the door.*
Sería Juan.  *It was probably Juan.*

Ana no fue a la fiesta.  *Ana did not go to the party.*
Estaría enferma.  *She was probably sick.*

**Exercise 12.** Conjugate the following verbs in the conditional tense.

1. yo (to go) _____
2. ellos (to put, place) _____
3. nosotros (to do, make) _____
4. mi papá (to leave) _____
5. tú (to send) _____
6. ustedes (to say, tell) _____
7. ella (to come) _____
8. usted (to leave) _____
9. yo (to give) _____
10. nosotros (to direct, conduct) _____

## Conditional Perfect

| Conditional Perfect Tense Conjugations: Regular Verbs | | |
|---|---|---|
| **Hablar** | **Comer** | **Vivir** |
| habría hablado | habría comido | habría vivido |
| habrías hablado | habrías comido | habrías vivido |
| habría hablado | habría comido | habría vivido |
| habríamos hablado | habríamos comido | habríamos vivido |
| habríais hablado | habríais comido | habríais vivido |
| habrían hablado | habrían comido | habrían vivido |

    The conditional perfect tense is formed by combining the conditional of the verb **haber** and the past participle. The conditional perfect is used to talk about an event that would have taken place if something had not prevented it from happening. As was the case with the conditional, the conditional perfect is often used in indirect discourse and may be used to express probability. This often equivalent to the English *had probably + past participle*.

Me dijo que habría comprado el carro, pero no tenía dinero.
*He told me that he would have bought the car, but he didn't have money.*

Yo no vi a Juan. Habría salido temprano.
*I didn't see Juan. He had probably left early.*

**Exercise 13.** Translate the following to English.

1. tú (would not go) _____
2. ella (will go) _____
3. ellos (would leave) _____
4. tú (would have written) _____
5. ella (had seen) _____
6. yo (will make) _____

7. yo (would have died) _____  
8. nosotros (had spoken) _____  
9. él (has gone) _____  
10. ustedes (will have left) _____  
11. ellos (would watch) _____  
12. yo (would have broken) _____  
13. ustedes (had gone to bed) _____  
14. ella (had put, placed) _____  
15. tú (will have returned) _____  
16. nosotros (will come) _____  
17. ellos (had made) _____  
18. ella (would have opened) _____  
19. yo (will get dressed) _____  
20. yo (had eaten) _____  

**Exercise 14.** Fill in the blank with the correctly conjugated form of the verb in parentheses.

1. Yo_____a la universidad, pero no tengo carro.   (would go)
2. Ellos_____a las siete mañana.   (will leave)
3. Él_____la comida en la mesa para las seis.   (will have put)
4. Ellos_____en la biblioteca mañana.   (are studying)
5. Tú_____una A, pero no estudiaste.   (would have received)
6. Ella_____el programa cuando llegué.   (had seen)
7. Usted_____la tarea, ¿no?   (will do)
8. Javier_____a la universidad hoy.   (is going)
9. Mi abuelo_____un carro feo.   (has)
10. Ellos_____.   (have died)
11. Yo_____los libros en mi carro.   (will put)
12. Ella_____la verdad, pero tenía miedo.   (would have told)
13. Juan_____la torta cuando llegamos.   (had made)
14. Anoche yo_____cuando mi papá llamó.   (was reading)
15. Él no vino a la fiesta anoche; él_____enfermo.   (must have been)
16. Ana_____la ventana con una piedra.   (has broken)
17. Sé que tú lo_____, pero no es necesario.   (would do)
18. Mi jefe no me_____el libro.   (has returned)
19. María y Marcos_____para las cinco.   (will have returned)
20. Cuando ella llamó, yo_____la tienda.   (had opened)

**Exercise 15.** Translate the following sentences to Spanish.

1. Have you finished your report?
_____

2. I would have done it, but I didn't have time.
_____

3. Besides, you told me that you never did your homework when you were young.
_____

4. When I told you that, you had not received a bad grade in history class.
_____

5. I always got good grades.
_____

6. That is not what Grandma told me. She says your teacher called every week.
_____

7. Grandma likes to gossip.
_____

8. Did Grandma also tell you that you won't be able to go out tomorrow if you have not finished your report?
_____
_____

9. Okay. I will have finished everything by 8:00 tonight. Grandma had probably forgotten that you were an excellent student.
_____
_____

10. When you learn that I am always right, I won't have to scold you.
_____

## Other Progressive Tenses

While the present progressive and the imperfect progressive tenses are used fairly often in Spanish, there are other progressive tenses which are not used nearly so frequently. These include the future, conditional, preterit, present perfect, and pluperfect progressive tenses. Their usage is similar to comparable tenses in English. Because they are used less frequently, particularly in spoken Spanish, these tenses will not be given much attention here. However, it does bear mentioning that the preterit progressive is distinguished from the imperfect progressive by the fact that it limits a past continuous action to a specific time period.

**Future progressive**

Esta noche estaré comiendo con mi familia.
*Tonight I will be eating with my family.*

**Conditional progressive**

Si hubiera ganado, estaría jugando al vólibol en una playa de Cancún.
*If I had won, I would be playing volleyball on a Cancun beach.*

**Preterit perfect progressive**

Estuve bailando por tres horas anoche.
*I was dancing for three hours last night.*

**Present perfect progressive**

Hemos estado estudiando mucho.
*We have been studying a lot.*

**Past perfect progressive**

Había estado practicando fútbol con mis amigos.
*I had been playing soccer with my friends.*

## Lexical Differences

**IR/IRSE/MARCHARSE/VENIR/DEJAR/SALIR**

**Ir-***to go (towards a specific place)*

| | |
|---|---|
| Yo voy al cine. | *I am going to the movies.* |
| Ellos fueron a la fiesta anoche. | *They went to the party last night.* |

**Irse-***to go away, leave*

With **irse** it is less likely that a specific place will be mentioned. In this sense the verb **irse** is equivalent to the verb **marcharse**.

| | |
|---|---|
| Ellos se fueron. | *They left.* |
| Me voy. | *I'm leaving.* |
| Habló con ellos y se marchó. | *He talked with them and left.* |

**Salir-***to leave*

This verb is used when one is leaving an enclosed place such as a house, school, or building. The verb **irse** may also be used in this sense, but with **irse** the departure is considered to be for a longer period of time. However, **salir** is also commonly used to talk about travel departures and modes of transportation. **Salir** can be used in the sense of *to go out* with someone.

| | |
|---|---|
| Voy a salir de la casa a las siete. | *I am going to leave the house at 7:00.* |
| Ella terminó su trabajo y se fue. | *She finished her work and left.* |
| Andrés no va a salir con ella. | *Andrés is not going to go out with her.* |
| El avión salió con dos horas de retraso. | *The plane left two hours late.* |

**Dejar-***to leave someone or something behind*

| | |
|---|---|
| Van a dejar una propina en la mesa. | *They are going to leave a tip on the table.* |
| Yo dejé a mis amigos en la fiesta. | *I left my friends at the party.* |

**Venir–***to come*

The verb **venir** indicates movement from a place and, in most cases, is equivalent to the English verb *to come*.

| | |
|---|---|
| ¡Ven acá! | *Come here!* |
| Todo el mundo está aquí. Debes venir. | *Everyone is here. You should come.* |

As mentioned above, the verb **ir** shows motion towards a place and is usually equivalent to the verb *to go* in English. However, there are some instances where Spanish usage of **ir** and **venir** differs from the English equivalents *to go* and *to come*. In order to determine whether **ir** or **venir** should be used in Spanish, one must consider the location of the speaker and the person spoken to. In Spanish **ir** is used to mean to move *away from* the place where the *speaker* is located. **Venir** is used to show movement *toward* the place where the *speaker* is located. The most problematic usage for English speakers involves cases where the verb *to come* is used in English to show movement away from the location of the speaker and toward the person spoken to. In this case, Spanish would require the verb **ir** rather than **venir**.

| | |
|---|---|
| Quiero que vengas a mi casa ahora. | *I want you to come to my house (where I am) now.* |
| No puedo ir ahora; tengo que estudiar. | *I can't come now; I have to study.* |
| Después de clase voy a tu casa. | *After class, I am coming to your house.* |
| Espera, ya voy. | *Wait, I'm coming (to where you are).* |
| ¿Quieres ir a México conmigo? | *Do you want to come to Mexico with me?* |

**Exercise 16.** Translate the following sentences to Spanish.

1. He would have gone to the game, but he was sick.

2. She was sleeping when we left.

3. Where have you put the tools?

4. She had still not called when they arrived.

5. I am bored. Why don't you come to visit me?

6. My parents have been living in this house for ten years.

7. I will have finished my homework by 7:00. Afterwards, I'm leaving.

8. Be patient! I'm coming.

9. My husband is generous. He always leaves a 7% tip for the waiter.

10. I have never been to Spain, but I'd like to go one day.

11. I will come to see you after I get dressed.

12. When we arrived at the house, she had already broken the window.

13. Her grandparents have told her that they are going to buy her a car.

14. We will turn off the lights before leaving.

15. I can't come to the office today; I'm sick.

# CHAPTER 2

# Nouns and Articles

## Number

Nouns are words that are used to refer to a person, place, thing, or idea. In Spanish, all nouns show grammatical gender; they will be either masculine or feminine. Nouns also show number; they are either singular or plural. With regard to number, the system for forming plurals in Spanish is fairly simple. Singular nouns ending in a vowel are made plural by adding **–s**. Nouns that end in a consonant, including **y**, are made plural by adding **–es**.

| libro | *book* | libros | *books* |
| actor | *actor* | actores | *actors* |

If a noun ends in **–z**, the plural is formed by changing the **z** to **c** and adding **-es**. Nouns ending in **–s** whose final vowel is unstressed will remain unchanged in the plural. If a word ends in an accented vowel other than **-é**, the plural is formed by adding **–es**. Some common exceptions to this rule are: **mamás** *'mothers'*, **papás** *'fathers'* or *'parents'*, **menús** *'menus'*, and **sofás** *'sofas'*.

| la luz | *light* | las luces | *lights* |
| el martes | *on Tuesday* | los martes | *on Tuesdays* |
| el análisis | *analysis* | los análisis | *analyses* |
| el tabú | *taboo* | los tabúes | *taboos* |
| el rubí | *ruby* | los rubíes | *rubies* |

**Exercise 1.** Make the following nouns plural.

1. el lápiz_____
2. la flor_____
3. el salvavidas_____
4. el reloj_____
5. la crisis_____
6. el hindú_____
7. el papá_____
8. el jueves_____
9. el peso_____
10. la voz_____
11. el lavaplatos_____
12. el café_____
13. la ley_____
14. la papa_____
15. el mapa_____
16. el paraguas_____
17. el francés_____
18. el domingo_____
19. el día_____
20. el sofá_____

# Gender

It is not difficult for English speakers to understand gender when the term is used in reference to nouns or pronouns that are generally considered to be either male or female, as is the case with people and some higher animals. With some nouns and pronouns such as *boy*, *girl*, *man*, *woman*, *he*, *she*, *mare*, *bull*, *ewe*, *buck*, and *doe*, English does clearly mark gender. On the other hand, gender is not marked in English for *child*, *student*, *it*, *they*, *you*, *horse*, *sheep* and *deer*.

In Spanish, however, gender is grammaticalized; all nouns are classified as either masculine or feminine. Thus, English-speaking students must become accustomed to learning and marking grammatical gender distinctions in Spanish. For purposes of memorizing vocabulary, it is suggested that students learn the lexical item along with its definite article. For example, rather than memorizing *pencil* as **lápiz**, students are advised to learn **el lápiz**. While this may at first seem to be a daunting task for beginning students, they soon learn that gender is fairly predictable in Spanish most of the time.

The most helpful rule in determining the gender of nouns holds that words which end in the letter **-o** are masculine, and words that end in the letter **-a** are feminine. Unfortunately, there are many exceptions to the -o rule, including such common expressions as **la mano** *'hand'*, **la foto** *'photo'*, etc. According to another well-known rule, words that end in the letters **-l**, **-n** and **-r**, are most often masculine. Among the common exceptions to this rule are **la piel** *'skin'*, **la sal** *'salt'*, and **la cárcel** *'jail'*.

The rule that words ending in the letter **-a** are generally feminine is not without its own exceptions, as evidenced by **el día** *'day'* **el mapa** *'map'*, and **el mañana** *'tomorrow'*. In fact, many words that end in **-ma** are derived from Greek and are masculine. However, there are also many feminine nouns that end in **-ma**, including **la cama** *'bed'*, **la goma** *'rubber'*, **la lágrima** *'tear'*, **la crema** *'cream'*, **la yema** *'egg yolk'*, etc.

| | | | |
|---|---|---|---|
| el aroma | *aroma* | el poema | *poem* |
| el fantasma | *ghost* | el problema | *problem* |
| el clima | *climate* | el sistema | *system* |
| el drama | *drama* | el telegrama | *telegram* |

Somewhat more reliable is the rule that words which end in **-ción**, **-sión**, **-dad**, **-tad**, **-tud**, **-umbre**, **-eza**, and **-nza** are feminine.

| | | | |
|---|---|---|---|
| la canción | *song* | la libertad | *liberty* |
| la certeza | *certainty* | la verdad | *truth* |
| la crisis | *crisis* | la versión | *version* |
| la esperanza | *hope* | la virtúd | *virtue* |

Some nouns referring to people have the same masculine and feminine forms. The article is changed according to the gender of the person.

| | | |
|---|---|---|
| el agente | la agente | *agent* |
| el artista | la artista | *artist* |
| el atleta | la atleta | *athlete* |
| el cantante | la cantante | *singer* |
| el juez | la juez | *judge* |

| | | |
|---|---|---|
| el modelo | la modelo | *model* |
| el testigo | la testigo | *witness* |

Nouns that end with **-ón, -ín, -or, –és, -d, -l, -y** or **–r** generally add an **–a** for the feminine form.

| | | |
|---|---|---|
| el doctor | la doctora | *doctor* |
| el huésped | la huéspeda | *guest* |
| el león | la leona | *lion* |
| el trabajador | la trabajadora | *worker* |

Many nouns in Spanish, particularly those that refer to people or animals, have entirely different words for each gender.

| | | |
|---|---|---|
| el gallo | la gallina | *rooster/hen* |
| el hombre | la mujer | *man/woman* |
| el rey | la reina | *king/queen* |
| el toro | la vaca | *bull/cow* |

Some nouns have only one gender. In these cases the noun retains the same gender regardless of whether its referent is male or female.

| | |
|---|---|
| el ángel | *angel* |
| el bebé | *baby* |
| la persona | *person* |
| la estrella | *TV/movie star* |
| la víctima | *victim* |

The days of the week, colors, numbers, as well as the names of mountains, oceans, and rivers are usually masculine.

| | |
|---|---|
| el miércoles | *Wednesday* |
| el Caribe | *the Caribbean* |
| el Everest | *(Mount) Everest* |
| el Amazonas | *the Amazon* |

Some words can be either masculine or feminine depending on meaning.

| | | | |
|---|---|---|---|
| el capital | *money* | la capital | *capital (of a country)* |
| el coma | *coma* | la coma | *comma* |
| el corte | *cut* | la corte | *court* |
| el cólera | *cholera* | la cólera | *anger* |
| el cura | *priest* | la cura | *cure* |
| el Papa | *Pope* | la papa | *potato* |
| el policía | *policeman* | la policía | *police force/policewoman* |
| el moral | *mulberry tree* | la moral | *morals* |

# Definite Articles

| | Forms of the Definite Article | |
|---|---|---|
| | Singular | Plural |
| Masculine | el libro | los libros |
| Feminine | la casa | las casas |

In general, the definite article in Spanish has four forms and must agree in gender and number with the noun it modifies. The masculine singular form **el** must be used before feminine singular nouns that begin with a stressed **á** sound. As the plural forms clearly show, the gender of the noun remains feminine. If the **a-** at the beginning of a word is not the stressed syllable, the feminine definite article is used, as with **la artista** *'artist'* and **la abeja** *'bee'*.

| | | | |
|---|---|---|---|
| el agua | *water* | las aguas | *waters* |
| el harpa | *harp* | las harpas | *harps* |
| el alma | *soul* | las almas | *souls* |
| el águila | *eagle* | las águilas | *eagles* |
| el aula | *classroom* | las aulas | *classrooms* |

**Exercise 2.** Translate the following to Spanish.

1. the pictures _____
2. the priest _____
3. the (female) witness _____
4. the hunger _____
5. the actress _____
6. the Pacific Ocean _____
7. the blue (of your eyes) _____
8. the hands _____
9. the papers _____
10. the (male) artist _____
11. the (male) professors _____
12. the (female) angel _____
13. the court _____
14. the (male) movie star _____
15. the (female) athlete _____
16. the water _____
17. the policeman _____
18. the tree _____
19. the parents _____
20. the honey _____
21. the eagles _____
22. the pencils _____

## Similar Uses of the Definite Article in Spanish and English

In Spanish and English the definite article is used to indicate a particular noun which functions as the subject, an object, or as a predicate noun. The main function of the definite article in both Spanish and English is to specify or limit nouns according to an identifying context previously known and understood by the speaker.

| | |
|---|---|
| El cuarto está sucio. | *The room is dirty.* |
| Dame el dinero. | *Give me the money.* |
| Juan es el chico que habla francés. | *Juan is the boy who speaks French.* |

In both Spanish and English, the indefinite article is used to introduce a noun into discourse. Once it is introduced, there is a switch to the definite article to maintain common focus.

| | |
|---|---|
| Conocí a una chica bonita anoche. | *I met a pretty girl last night.* |
| La chica bailó conmigo. | *The girl danced with me.* |

Given the right context, shared culture, or focus of attention as is the case with **el sol, el profesor, el tren**, etc., Whitley (1986: 155) points out that it is not necessary to use an indefinite article to introduce a noun into the context.

| | |
|---|---|
| ¿A qué hora llega el tren? | *What time does the train arrive?* |
| En este imperio nunca se pone el sol. | *The sun never sets on this empire.* |

Definite articles are used in Spanish to refer generally to all members of an entire class. Totality may be understood in terms of the "generic whole" or a "whole class or species." In English this sometimes occurs with singular count nouns used in a generic sense.

| | |
|---|---|
| El perro es un mamífero. | *The dog is a mammal.* |
| El martillo es una herramienta. | *The hammer is a tool.* |
| La computadora ha cambiado el mundo. | *The computer has changed the world.* |

## Differences in Definite Article Usage

In Spanish the infinitive functions as a noun. In sentence-initial position the definite article often precedes the infinitive. This meaning is rendered in English by the gerund.

| | |
|---|---|
| El estudiar es muy importante. | *Studying is very important.* |
| El fumar es muy peligroso. | *Smoking is very dangerous.* |

The days of the week are all masculine in Spanish. With days of the week, Spanish uses the definite article except after the verb **ser**. In a complete sentence, the definite article is also used with dates.

| | |
|---|---|
| Quiero ir al cine el sábado. | *I want to go to the movies on Saturday.* |
| No tenemos clase los martes. | *We don't have class on Tuesdays.* |

| | |
|---|---|
| ¡Hasta el viernes! | *See you on Friday!* |
| Hoy es jueves. | *Today is Thursday.* |
| El accidente ocurrió el tres de mayo. | *The accident occurred on May third.* |

The definite article rather than the possessive adjective is used with articles of clothing and parts of the body in most cases, particularly in sentences in which reflexive verbs are used.

| | |
|---|---|
| Me lavé las manos. | *I washed my hands.* |
| Se quitó los zapatos. | *She took off her shoes.* |

The definite article is used before specific meals. The verb **tomar** is preferred by many Spanish speakers when talking about eating a particular meal.

| | |
|---|---|
| Vamos a tomar el desayuno. | *We are going to have breakfast.* |
| Tengo que preparar la cena. | *I have to prepare dinner.* |

The definite article is used before titles when talking about the person whose title is being used. When speaking directly to someone, no article is used. The article is not used before the titles **don**, **doña**, **san**, **santo**, **santa**, and **fray**. To talk about an entire family, the masculine plural definite article is also used before surnames.

| | |
|---|---|
| El señor Fernández no vive en esa casa. | *Mr. Fernández does not live in that house.* |
| Buenos días, Doctora Rodriguez. | *Good morning, Doctor Rodriguez.* |
| Doña Marta es mi vecina. | *Ms. Marta is my neighbor.* |
| Fui a visitar a los Lorca. | *I went to visit the the Lorcas.* |

With the verbs **aprender**, **entender**, **comprender**, **enseñar**, **leer**, and some other verbs relating to language, the article is optional. However, if an adverb is used between the verb and the name of the language, the article is required.

Hablé (el) francés con mis amigos anoche.
*I spoke French with my friends last night.*

Hablaba frecuentemente el español cuando vivía en Dallas.
*I frequently spoke Spanish when I lived in Dallas.*

In Spanish and in English, the definite article usually accompanies a prepositional object referring to a location. Students sometimes have problems with a few common cases where English does not require a definite article. The definite article is usually omitted with some common place names such as **clase** and **casa** when they are preceded by the prepositions **en**, **a**, and **de**.

| | |
|---|---|
| Voy a la universidad. | *I am going to the university.* |
| La vimos en la televisión. | *We saw her on television.* |
| Lo llevaron a la cárcel. | *They took him to jail.* |
| Salimos para la iglesia a las nueve. | *We leave for church at nine.* |
| Los niños están en la escuela. | *The children are at school.* |

Vamos a clase.　　　　　　　　　　　　*We are going to class.*
Ellos están en casa.　　　　　　　　　*They are at home.*

**Exercise 3.** Fill in the blank with the correct form of the definite article, if needed.

1. Tienen que limpiar_____apartamento_____lunes.
2. Voy a tomar_____desayuno antes de salir.
3. Ellos piensan pagar la multa porque no quieren ir a_____cárcel.
4. Mi jefe no pudo resolver_____problema.
5. No estoy bien. Voy a hablar con_____doctor García.
6. Ella se puso_____zapatos y se fue.
7. _____español es una materia interesante.
8. Fui al cine con_____Doña Marta.
9. Hoy es_____viernes.
10. Ella se rompió_____brazo.
11. No sé dónde está_____ reloj que compré ayer.
12. Ella quiere ver_____ave que está en_____árbol.
13. Buenos días, _____señorita Pacheco.
14. Ellos trabajan_____jueves.
15. Habla_____francés, pero no ha viajado a Francia.
16. ¡Hasta_____miércoles!
17. Yo tuve que ir a_____iglesia antes.
18. Ella aprendió bien_____español.
19. Necesito quitarme_____suéter.
20. No quiero llegar tarde a_____clase.

**The Definite Article with Generic Reference**

　　　　With regard to definite article usage, the major difference between the two languages has to do with the fact that Spanish consistently and systematically uses the definite article to mark totality, while English does so very rarely. Count nouns must have an article to denote all members of their class. In other words, to refer to all of something, to an entire class, or to a noun in an abstract, general, or universal sense, Spanish uses the definite article, whereas English tends to avoid it.

Los perros son inteligentes.　　　　　　*Dogs are intelligent.*
Los caballos son interesantes.　　　　　*Horses are interesting.*

The definite article is used for nouns of generic reference.

| | |
|---|---|
| Me gustan los gatos. | *I like cats.* |
| Los hombres son mortales. | *Men are mortal.* |
| Los perros son muy fieles. | *Dogs are very faithful.* |

Because Spanish always marks the generic whole by using the definite article, there are often cases where isolated sentences would be ambiguous.

| | |
|---|---|
| Los estudiantes son trabajadores. | *Students are hardworking (in general).* |
| | *The students (in this particular group) are hardworking.* |

Even non-count (mass) nouns which refer to an idea or substance generally require the definite article.

| | |
|---|---|
| El azúcar es un producto importante. | *Sugar is an important product.* |
| La educación es esencial. | *Education is essential.* |
| El trabajo es bueno para el alma. | *Work is good for the soul.* |

One of the major difficulties students have with article usage in Spanish involves being able to distinguish a noun which is being used in an abstract or general sense from a noun which refers not to the whole of its class, but to a certain part of this whole. In the latter case, the noun is being used in a partitive sense; the definite article is not used before nouns that are used in this way.

| | |
|---|---|
| Tiene suerte. | La suerte controla la vida. |
| *He is lucky.* | *Luck controls life.* |
| | |
| Necesito dinero. | El dinero es necesario. |
| *I need (some) money.* | *Money is necessary.* |
| | |
| ¿Tienes leche? | La leche es una bebida deliciosa. |
| *Do you have (any) milk?* | *Milk is a delicious drink.* |
| | |
| Como pan por la mañana. | Me gusta el pan. |
| *I eat (some) bread in the morning.* | *I like bread.* |
| | |
| Bebemos cerveza. | La cerveza es cara. |
| *We are drinking (some) beer.* | *Beer is expensive.* |
| | |
| Francia exporta vino. | El vino es un producto importante de Francia. |
| *France exports wine.* | *Wine is an important product of France.* |

**Exercise 4.** Fill in the blank with the correct form of the definite article, if needed.

1. _____ vida es muy corta.
2. _____ señor Ruiz dice que _____ postres son malos para _____ salud.
3. Sin embargo, _____ doña Luisa dice que él come _____ chocolate todos los días.
4. Ayer compramos _____ carne, pero no tenían _____ carne que tú pediste.
5. ¿Te gusta _____ té?
6. _____ inglés es más difícil que _____ español, pero hablo mejor _____ inglés.
7. Nosotros fuimos a _____ escuela ayer.
8. Hoy es _____ martes.
9. Vamos a servir _____ pescado en la fiesta mañana. A Ana le gusta _____ pescado.
10. Ella comió _____ pollo que yo había comprado para esta noche.
11. Yo fui a Target para comprar _____ lámparas.
12. En ese restaurante venden _____ sándwiches deliciosos.
13. Nosotros pensamos llegar a España para _____ jueves.
14. Necesito mucho dinero para comprar _____ caviar porque _____ caviar es muy caro.
15. Hoy en día _____ mantas que fabrican no son de buena calidad.


**Exercise 5.** Translate the following sentences to Spanish.

1. She left for school at 8:00 in the morning.
_____

2. We need to buy wine and cheese for dinner.
_____

3. They always go to church on Sundays.
_____

4. I am not going to see them until Friday.
_____

5. He washed his hands before eating.
_____

6. Everyone knows that love is blind.
___

7. The doctor at the clinic says that water is necessary for the human body.
___

8. We met Mr. García's daughter at school.
___

9. Single women are smarter than married women.
___

10. They need the book that we bought yesterday.
___

## Nominalization

**Definite Article + Adjective**

In Spanish definite articles may be used with adjectives to create noun phrases. In these cases the definite article and the adjective agree in gender and number with the noun they are replacing.

A Marta le gustan estos zapatos, pero yo quiero comprar los rojos.
*Marta likes these shoes, but I want to buy the red ones.*

El come una banana verde. Yo prefiero las maduras.
*He is eating a green banana. I prefer the ripe ones.*

**Definite Article + que**

Cases like *the one(s) which/who . . . .* or *those (of us, of you, etc.) who . . . .* are generally expressed by the definite article and **que**. These nominalized forms also have a specific referent and will agree in gender and number with the nouns they replace.

¿Cuál es tu paraguas? ¿El que está afuera?
*Which one is your umbrella? The one that is outside?*

Queremos llevar a los niños buenos. Los que se comportan mal no van.
*We want to take good children. Those who behave badly won't go.*

¿Quieres comprar este mantel? No, busco el que tiene flores.
*Do you want to buy this tablecloth? No, I am looking for the one that has flowers.*

**Lo + Adjective**

In Spanish the neuter article **lo** can also be used to nominalize adjectives. When used in this way, these adjectives do not have a specific referent but are used in an abstract sense. This expression is very often equivalent to the English expressions *the (good, bad, interesting, etc.) thing*.

Lo bueno es que estudian mucho. *The good thing is that they study a lot.*
Lo importante es que tienes más tiempo. *The important thing is that you have more time.*

**Lo que**

The neuter **lo** may be used with the relative **que** without reference to any particular noun. In this case the meaning is equivalent to the English *what* or *the thing that*.

Lo que necesito es más dinero. *What I need is more money.*
Lo que quiere es estar sola. *What she wants is to be alone.*

**Exercise 6.** Translate the following sentences to Spanish.

1. She buys vegetables at the market near her house.

2. The sad thing is that they never see their grandchildren.

3. Do you want this ice cream? No, I want the big one that you are hiding.

4. What bothers me is your attitude.

5. She prefers used cars, but I am going to buy the new one.

6. Well, the scary thing is that he does not have a helmet.

7. We need some pillows for the bed we bought on Friday.

8. If you want my opinion, she is the guilty one.

9. He always sells eggs at this market.

_____

10. She does not like horror movies; she prefers romantic ones.

_____

## Indefinite Articles

| Forms of the Indefinite Article | | |
|---|---|---|
| | **Singular** | **Plural** |
| **Masculine** | **un** libro | **unos** libros |
| **Feminine** | **una** casa | **unas** casas |

As has already been pointed out, the indefinite article is often used to introduce a noun into a discussion. Once the noun has been introduced, it will usually be modified by the definite article. As was the case with the definite article, the masculine singular indefinite article is used before feminine singular nouns that begin with stressed **á** or **ha**. Thus, one would have, for example, **un águila** and **un arpa**, but **unas águilas** and **unas arpas**.

| | |
|---|---|
| Tráeme un libro. | *Bring me a book.* |
| Aquí tienes el libro que pediste. | *Here is the book that you asked for.* |

Both English and Spanish sometimes drop the indefinite article with non-count nouns and plural count nouns.

| | |
|---|---|
| Ana come pan. | *Ana is eating (some) bread.* |
| Marcos is drinking (some) wine. | *Marcos bebe vino.* |
| Juan compra (unos) libros. | *John is buying (some) books.* |
| María hace (unas) tortillas. | *María is making (some) tortillas.* |
| Ellos no tienen hijos. | *They don't have (any) children.* |

However, the indefinite article is used more often in English than in Spanish. A major difference with regard to indefinite article usage in Spanish and English has to do with the fact that Spanish sometimes does not use indefinite articles with singular count nouns. This can be attributed to the fact that in Spanish **un** retains its numerical value of *one*. For this reason, in cases where the speaker is not selecting one and only one but is instead referring indefinitely to an unqualified member of the group, the indefinite article is not used. Omission of the indefinite article signifies that the noun is being used for its sense alone without reference to a particular individual.

In general, the indefinite article is omitted in Spanish if the speaker simply wishes to identify the noun. If one only wants to talk about the existence versus nonexistence of someone or something without wanting to individualize it, single it out, or emphasize it, no indefinite article is used in Spanish. So, with verbs that refer fundamentally to existence such as **tener** and **haber**, the indefinite article is often omitted, particularly when the concept of quantity is not emphasized. This is often the case with verbs like **llevar**, **usar**, and **necesitar** when the assumption is that a person would have, wear, or need only one of these items at a time.

| | |
|---|---|
| El hombre lleva sombrero. | *The man is wearing a hat.* |
| Tomás no tiene novia. | *Tomás does not have a girlfriend.* |
| El perro no tiene cola. | *The dog does not have a tail.* |
| No tengo carro. | *I don't have a car.* |

Spanish does not use the indefinite article after the verb **ser** with unmodified noun that refers to profession, religion, nationality, or marital status. However, if the adjective or adjective phrase is considered to be an integral part of the noun, no article is used even though the noun is modified.

| | |
|---|---|
| Marcos es protestante. | *Marcos is (a) Protestant.* |
| Ella es abogada. | *She is a lawyer.* |
| ¿Tú eres mexicana? | *Are you Mexican?* |
| Juan es un profesor excelente. | *Juan is an excellent professor.* |
| Es una enfermera que tiene compasión. | *She is a nurse who has compassion.* |
| Soy profesor de español. | *I am a Spanish professor.* |

The indefinite article is generally omitted before **cierto**, **cien**, **mil**, **otro**, and **medio**.

| | |
|---|---|
| Necesito otro tenedor. | *I need another fork* |
| Vivieron aquí por mil años. | *They lived here for a thousand years.* |

**Exercise 7.** Fill in the blank with the correct form of the indefinite article, if needed.

1. Jorge es _____ arquitecto.

2. Rafael es _____ hombre interesante.

3. No tengo _____ bicicleta.

4. Juana es _____ protestante muy devota.

5. Tengo que buscar _____ otra mochila.

6. El chico tiene _____ pierna rota.

7. Jorge es _____ cantante mexicano.

8. El hombre que robó la tienda tenía _____ bigote.

9. Juana compró _____ vestido azul.

10. Juan tenía _____ cabeza enorme.

11. Prefiero salir sin _____ abrigo.

12. Ana es _____ maestra talentosa.

13. Mi amiga vive en_____ barrio pequeño cerca del parque.

14. Quiero que compres_____ media docena de huevos.

15. Marcos va a traerme_____ vaso de jugo.

**Exercise 8.** Translate the following to Spanish.

1. My brother is a commercial pilot.

2. He has a plane that he bought in Spain last year.

3. What I want is to travel to Europe by ship.

4. Porfirio Díaz was a Mexican who fought against the French.

5. Pain does not bother me unless I have a headache.

6. Salvador Dalí is a famous painter.

7. She is looking for a certain bottle of wine.

8. The man that talked with us is a Catholic.

9. They always walk because they don't have a car.

10. My mother made us a cake for the party.

## Lexical Differences

### ¿QUÉ?/¿CUÁL(CUÁLES)?

**¿Qué? -what**

The interrogative **¿qué?** may be used to ask for a definition.

| | |
|---|---|
| ¿Qué es un pachanguero? | *What is a pachanguero?* |
| ¿Qué es eso? | *What is that?* |

**¿Cuál? (Cuáles)?**-*which?, which one(s)?*

These interrogative expressions usually ask for a choice of alternatives. They are sometimes used with the preposition **de** and the definite article to indicate such a choice.

| | |
|---|---|
| ¿Cuál es tu nombre? | *What is your name?* |
| ¿Cuál es la fecha? | *What is the date?* |
| ¿Cuál de los dos libros prefieres? | *Which of the two books do you prefer?* |

However, this explanation of interrogative use is not always clear to students since **¿qué?** is used in some situations in which a choice among alternatives appears to be needed.

| | |
|---|---|
| ¿Qué fecha es hoy? | *What is the date today?* |
| ¿Qué día es hoy? | *What day is today?* |

A good rule of thumb is that one should use **¿qué?** before nouns when the intended meaning is *which?* While **¿cuál?** may be used in this way in some parts of Latin America, this usage is rejected by many native speakers.

| | |
|---|---|
| ¿Qué libro prefieres? | *Which book do you prefer?* |
| ¿Qué película quieres ver? | *Which movie do you want to see?* |

**Exercise 9.** Fill in the blank with the correct definite article or with the Spanish expression needed to translate the English expression in parentheses. In cases where no definite article is needed, place an X in the blank.

1. Vamos al correo porque necesitamos comprar_____sellos.

2. Para mantener una dieta vegetariana, _____legumbres son esenciales.

3. Tienes que recordar que_____paciencia es una virtud.

4. Tenía que ir a_____escuela todos los días.

5. _____ es que no saben leer. (The ridiculous thing)

6. Mañana es _____ tres de agosto.

7. _____ ejercicio es necesario para _____ gatos.

8. Colombia perdió _____ dinero porque _____ café es su producto principal.

9. No tengo mucha hambre; sólo voy a comer _____ pan esta noche.

10. Esa tienda vende _____ manzanas.

11. Anoche fuimos a ver a _____ señorita Jimenez.

12. _____ doña María no viene a la casa mañana.

13. Los estudiantes se sorprendieron al ver _____ águila bonita.

14. _____ es que no llevaban ropa. (The funny thing)

15. Estos estudiantes salieron bien; _____ siempre estudian. (The smart ones)

**Exercise 10.** Fill in the blank with the correct form of the indefinite article, if needed. If no article is needed, put an X in the blank.

1. Mi cuñado es de Guadalajara; es _____ mexicano. (a)

2. Quiero _____ libro; éste no me gusta. (another)

3. Juan no gana mucho dinero porque es _____ profesor. (a)

4. Mi papá es _____ médico talentoso. (a)

5. Hay _____ abogada que vive en nuestro barrio. (a certain)

6. Mi hermana no cocina porque no tiene _____ estufa. (a)

7. Esa señora tiene _____ alma muy buena. (a)

8. Juan es _____ persona muy ocupada. (a)

**Exercise 11.** Translate the following to Spanish.

1. What is a picnic?
_____

2. It is a custom of eating outdoors. In my country picnics are very popular.
_____

3. What we need is another blanket.

___

4. Which of these desserts are you going to eat?

___

5. I am going to eat the chocolate one.

___

6. Sweets don't agree with me.

___

7. Don't you want to eat some cake?

___

8. Yes, but I don't have a fork.

___

9. You can eat it with your hands, if you want.

___

10. I didn't realize that you liked to eat outdoors.

___

# CHAPTER 3

# Pronouns

## Subject Pronouns

| | Subject Pronouns | |
|---|---|---|
| | **Singular** | **Plural** |
| 1st person | yo | nosotros, nosotras |
| 2nd person | tú | vosotros, vosotras |
| 3rd person | él, ella, usted | ellos, ellas, ustedes |

Pronouns are used to replace or refer back to someone or something that has already been mentioned or is understood from the context. The person, thing, or idea that is replaced by the pronoun is its antecedent. In the sentences below, Ana is the antecedent of the subject pronoun *she*, and *keys* is the antecedent of the direct object pronoun *them*.

*Ana is learning Spanish. She wants to visit Mexico.*

*Do you have my keys? No, I haven't seen them.*

Although not all grammarians categorize pronouns in exactly the same way, most would agree that the Spanish pronouns include subject, direct object, indirect object, demonstrative, prepositional, possessive, reflexive, relative, indefinite, and interrogative pronouns. Because the verb ending signals the person of a verb in Spanish, the subject pronoun can be omitted in Spanish, particularly when the referent is made clear by context. For this reason, Spanish is known as a *pro-drop language*, meaning that one can "drop" the subject pronoun.

| | |
|---|---|
| Soy americano. | *I am an American.* |
| Eres inteligente. | *You (familiar) are intelligent.* |

Since it is not necessary to fill this subject position with a pronoun, the dummy proform *it* is omitted in Spanish sentences where there is no real referent. With "impersonal verbs" such as **llover** and **nevar**, a subject pronoun is not used.

| | |
|---|---|
| Es interesante. | *It is interesting.* |
| Hace calor. | *It is hot.* |
| Llueve mucho. | *It is raining a lot.* |

English speakers often overuse the subject pronouns in Spanish. Subject pronouns may be used for emphasis or clarification, as in the first sentence below, but consistently using subject pronouns gives too much emphasis to the subject. It would be somewhat similar to using the same subject pronoun repeatedly in the second example below.

Ella puede ir si quiere, pero yo me quedo aquí.
*She can go if she wants, but **I'm** staying here.*

Yo me levanté a las siete, yo desayuné, y yo salí para el trabajo.
***I** got up at 7:00, **I** ate breakfast, and **I** left for work.*

## Other Uses of Subject Pronouns

The idea of *It is . . . .(I, you, he, she, we, they)* is expressed in Spanish by using the construction **ser + subject pronoun**. The verb **ser** will agree with the subject pronoun that follows it.

| | |
|---|---|
| ¿Quién puso la comida en la mesa? | *Who put the food on the table?* |
| Fui yo, mamá. | *It was I, mom.* |
| | |
| ¿Quién va a pagarme? | *Who is going to pay me?* |
| Son ellos que te deben pagar. | *It is they who should pay you.* |

If one wishes to use expressions such as *we men, you women,* etc., the subject pronoun *and the definite article* are used before the noun in Spanish.

Nosotros los chicos estudiamos más que ustedes las chicas.
*We boys study more than you girls.*

Ustedes los abogados son muy honrados y trabajadores.
*You lawyers are very honest and hardworking.*

## Formal and Informal

The system of classifying pronouns by person, 1st person (person speaking), 2nd person (person spoken to) and 3rd person (person spoken about), is complicated in Spanish by the fact that the pronouns **usted** and **ustedes** have third-person grammatical forms even though they mean *you (singular)* and *you (plural)*, respectively. This system is also more difficult for English speakers to understand because Spanish has the formal/informal distinction of **tú/usted** and **vosotros/ustedes**. As a general rule, one might say that the **tú/vosotros** forms are used with friends, family, close acquaintances or people with whom one would be on a first-name basis. The **usted/ustedes** forms, on the other hand, are used to show politeness or deference.

However, this is actually an oversimplification of the "rules" that govern the use of these pronouns of address in Spanish. Historically, Spanish had **tú** as the singular intimate form, with **vos** serving as both the singular and plural polite form, as is the case with modern French *tu* and *vous*. In order to distinguish its plural meaning, the plural **vos** was changed to **vosotros**. Over time, the formal or polite aspect of **vos** and **vosotros** was lost, and **vos** joined **tú** as an informal singular form. On the model of **nosotros/nosotras**, **vosotros/vosotras** came to be the plural informal address forms.

A new pair of polite address forms evolved from the historically third-person phrases **vuestra merced** and **vuestras mercedes**. These became the third-person singular **usted** and **ustedes** of modern Spanish. The use of **vosotros** gradually declined in southern Spain and most of Latin America. However, the singular **vos** form is still used in many areas of Latin America. In places where one finds both **tú** and **vos**, the system regulating appropriate usage is often difficult for outsiders to master. Choosing whether to use **tú**, **vos**, or **usted** can be a very complicated task in some cases.

## Prepositional Pronouns

| Prepositional Pronouns | |
|---|---|
| **Singular** | **Plural** |
| mí | nosotros, nosotras |
| ti | vosotros, vosotras |
| él, ella, usted | ellos, ellas, ustedes |

Prepositional pronouns are used after prepositions. However, the prepositions **entre** *'between'* or *'among'*, **según**, *'according to'*, **incluso** *'including'*, as well as **excepto**, **menos**, and **salvo** (all meaning *'except'*) take subject pronouns in the first and second-person singular. The preposition **con** is combined with the first-person singular or second-person singular prepositional pronouns to give the forms **conmigo** *'with me'* and **contigo**, *'with you'*. The form **consigo** *'with himself, herself, themselves"* is also sometimes used.

| | |
|---|---|
| Los regalos son para mí. | *The gifts are for me.* |
| Te dio el dinero a ti. | *He gave the money to you.* |
| No hablan de nosotros. | *They are not talking about us.* |
| Yo voy contigo. | *I am going with you.* |
| Ella habla conmigo. | *She is speaking with me.* |
| Según tú, todo está bien. | *According to you, everything is fine.* |

**Exercise 1.** Fill in the the word(s) necessary to translate the English expressions in parentheses.

1. _____ (It) es necesario que ella vaya _____ (with me).

2. ¿Quíen es el culpable? _____ (It is I.)

3. Yo conozco a los Ramírez. _____ (They) son muy amables.

4. _____ (You doctors) no ganan mucho dinero.

5. Todos fueron menos_____ (you), Marcos.

6. ¿Quiere_____ (you) más sopa, señor?

7. Ella no va a salir sin _____ (me).

8. _____ (She) no está hablando de_____ (you, familiar).

9. Tus padres están muy enojados_____ (with you), Daniel.

10. Según_____ (him), debemos salir temprano.

11. _____ (we) sabemos que el alquiler es muy caro para _____ (you, plural).

12. _____ (We students) tenemos que hacer la tarea.

13. _____ (You) hablas mucho, Juan.

14. Entre_____ (you) _____ (me), Javier, no me gusta la clase.

15. Esta torta no es para_____ (you), mi hijo.

**Exercise 2.** Translate the following sentences to Spanish.

1. It rains a lot in the winter.

_____

2. Juana is looking for the broom. She can't find it.

_____

3. It's not fair. We girls always have to clean the house.

_____

4. Our aunt prefers to stay here with you (informal).

_____

5. It is you (plural) who are sick.

_____

6. I found your keys? They are on the table.

_____

7. Do you want them to bring you the bill, Mr. García?

_____

8. If you want to go, you can call Mrs. Gonzáles.

_____

9. It bothers me that they spend so much money.

_____

10. You (plural) are going to invite your friends, right?

_____

11. They brought the wine for me.

_____

12. Everyone had a good time except me.

_____

13. Between you and me, I don't think she is joking.

_____

14. You students have too much free time.

_____

15. She says she doesn't want to put on makeup.

_____

# Object Pronouns

**Direct Object Pronouns**

| Direct Object Pronouns | |
|---|---|
| Singular | Plural |
| me | nos |
| te | os |
| lo, la | los, las |

The direct object pronoun refers to or substitutes for the person or thing that receives the action of the verb. Because it replaces a direct object, the direct object pronoun answers the question: "Whom or what receives the action?" Direct object pronouns agree in gender and number with the nouns they replace.

| | | |
|---|---|---|
| Ellos leen el libro. | *They are reading the book.* | (What are they reading?) |
| Ellos lo leen. | *They are reading it.* | |
| Conoce a la chica. | *He knows the girl.* | (Whom does he know?) |
| La conoce. | *He knows her.* | |

**Indirect Object Pronouns**

| Indirect Object Pronouns | |
|---|---|
| Singular | Plural |
| me | nos |
| te | os |
| le | les |

Unlike the direct object pronouns, the indirect object pronouns do not show gender in the third person forms. Indirect object pronouns most often answer the question: "To whom or for whom is the action done?"

Yo le di un regalo a mi papá.
*I gave a gift to my dad.*            (To whom did I give it?)

Le lavé el carro a mi amigo.
*I washed the car for my friend.*            (For whom did I wash it?)

However, there are many other possible ways in which the Spanish indirect object pronouns may be translated in English. An indirect object pronoun may be used in Spanish to show that a noun is somehow "involved" in the action of the sentence in a variety of ways. Butt and Benjamin (110-11) list numerous sentences which clearly show that the English expressions needed to translate them are far more varied than the typical *to whom or for whom something is done*. The following are but three of their examples.

| | |
|---|---|
| Le están sacando una muela. | *They are taking one of his teeth out.* |
| Le he comprado un cuadro. | *I have bought a picture from him.* |
| Le echaron una sábana. | *They threw a sheet over him.* |

The indirect object pronoun is used with **pedir**, **contestar**, **decir**, and **preguntar**.

| | |
|---|---|
| Les dijo la verdad. | *She told them the truth.* |
| Le pedí dinero a mi papá. | *I asked my father for money.* |
| Ellos le preguntaron cómo se llamaba. | *They asked him what his name was.* |

**Position of Object Pronouns**

As a general rule, direct and indirect object pronouns may precede the conjugated verb, or they may be attached to an infinitive or progressive form. Object pronouns must be attached to affirmative commands, and they must precede negative commands.

| | |
|---|---|
| Les gusta el carro. Van a comprarlo. | *They like the car. They are going to buy it.* |
| Dame las tortillas. Las quiero comer. | *Give me the tortillas. I want to eat them.* |
| Yo preparé la comida. ¡Cómela! | *I prepared the food. Eat it!* |
| ¡No me digas eso! | *Don't tell me that.* |

However, Solé and Solé maintain (1977: 95-96) that the pronouns may not be attached to an infinitive that is intransitive or to an auxiliary that is reflexive. They provide the following examples to illustrate this point.

| | |
|---|---|
| Le permitió volver. | *He allowed her to return.* |
| *Permitió volverle. | |
| | |
| Se puso a cantar. | *She began to sing.* |
| *Puso a cantarse. | |

On the other hand, Butt and Benjamin (1988:128) use the following examples to point out that the object pronouns must be attached to the infinitive if the verb is an affirmative command or if any other word intervenes between the verb phrase and the infinitive.

| | |
|---|---|
| Procura hacerlo. | *Try to do it.* |
| *Lo procura hacer. | |
| | |
| Trató varias veces de hacerlo. | *He tried several times to do it.* |
| *Lo trató varias veces de hacer. | |

## The Redundant Construction

Spanish speakers sometimes use pronouns where they seem to be "redundant" in that they add no new information to the sentence. It has already been noted that prepositional pronouns may be used with indirect object pronouns and direct object pronouns for purposes of clarification or emphasis. However, for many students the most troublesome case of "redundancy" in the use of pronouns has to do with the fact that English speakers may use either an indirect object or an indirect object pronoun in a particular sentence, but they would not use both in the same sentence.

| | |
|---|---|
| *We gave them the gifts.* | (indirect object pronoun) |
| *We gave our friends the gifts.* | (indirect object) |
| *\*We gave them our friends the gifts.* | (incorrect) |

However, in Spanish both an indirect object pronoun and and indirect object which have the same referent are often used together in the same sentence. This seemingly redundant use of the pronoun is confusing to many English speakers.

| | |
|---|---|
| Le di el dinero a Marcos. | *I gave the money to Marcos.* |
| Le va a mandar el regalo a su mamá. | *He is going to send the gift to his mother.* |

There is actually some disagreement among both native speakers and grammarians as to the acceptability of omitting the indirect object pronoun in sentences similar to first example given below. However, in cases such as the second example below, omission of the pronoun would be considered unacceptable by almost all native speakers. In sentences where the indirect object is a proper name, the indirect object pronoun is always used. As a general rule, the best advice for students is to use indirect object pronouns in Spanish sentences which have an indirect object.

| | |
|---|---|
| Doy dinero a mis amigos | *I give money to my friends.* |
| *Regaló un carro a mí. | *She gave me a car.* |
| Mándale el regalo a Juan. | *Send the gift to Juan.* |

## The Indirect Object Pronoun Versus Para

According to Iglesias and Meiden (1995: 62), the use of either an indirect object pronoun or **para + prepositional phrase** is acceptable if a concrete object is being exchanged between the parties involved. However, in cases where it is a service that is being rendered, only the indirect object pronoun should be used. While it is unlikely that there would be universal agreement among native speakers about the acceptability of **para + prepositional phrase** in the last two examples below, use of the indirect object pronoun would likely be considered the "safer" choice in these cases.

| | |
|---|---|
| Juan me compró un libro. | *Juan bought me a book.* |
| Juan compró un libro para mí. | |

| | |
|---|---|
| Mi esposa me trajo un regalo. | *My wife brought a gift for me.* |
| Mi esposa trajo un regalo para mí. | |
| | |
| Ana me lavó el carro. | *Ana washed the car for me.* |
| *Ana lavó el carro para mí. | |
| | |
| Tomás les abrió la puerta. | *Tomás opened the door for them.* |
| *Tomás abrió la puerta para ellos. | |

**Double Object Pronouns**

If both a direct object pronoun and an indirect object pronoun are used in the same sentence, the indirect object pronoun precedes the direct object pronoun. If a third person indirect object pronoun precedes a third person direct object pronoun, the indirect object pronoun becomes **se**.

| The Indirect Object Pronoun Se | | | |
|---|---|---|---|
| **le** and **les** | become **SE** | when they precede | **lo** **la** **los** **las** |

| | |
|---|---|
| ¿El dinero? Ellos me lo dieron. | *The money? They gave it to me.* |
| No tengo la carta. Te la mandé ayer. | *I don't have the letter. I sent it to you yesterday.* |
| Le compré un regalo a María. | *I bought a gift for Mary.* |
| Se lo di anoche. | *I gave it to her last night.* |
| ¿Van a mandarles la carta? | *Are you going to send them the letter?* |
| Sí, vamos a mandársela. | *Yes, we are going to send it to them.* |

**Exercise 3.** Fill in the blank with the equivalent Spanish expressions.

1. Ella siempre_____da dinero a su novio.   (him)
2. No encuentro mis llaves. Yo_____voy a buscar en mi carro.   (them)
3. El regalo es para_____.   (you, familiar)
4. Para_____, la historia es muy interesante.   (me)
5. Ella quiere ese carro. Su papá_____ _____va a dar.   (it, to her)
6. Ellos van a ir al cine_____.   (with me)
7. Ellos_____van a ver mañana.   (you, familiar)
8. Usted_____mandó una carta a su abuela, ¿no?   (her)
9. _____profesores trabajamos mucho.   (We)

10. ¿Quién habla? _____. (It's me.)

11. _____ muy difícil encontrar trabajo aquí. (It's)

12. Nuestros amigos van al cine_____. (with us)

13. Yo sé que_____eres muy inteligente. (you, familiar)

14. Ellos_____visitan todos los días, Señora Martínez. (you)

15. No quiero pedir_____dinero ahora. (him)

**Exercise 4.** Translate the following sentences to Spanish.

1. Did you buy the stamps? Yes, I gave them to you.

2. I brought you a dessert, but I ate it before giving it to you.

3. She never sends them photos of me.

4. We told her that she needs to take them to the park.

5. If you want me to remember that, you need to write it down for me.

6. I don't have your shoes, Juan. Look for them.

7. We showed her the necklace, but she said that she didn't like it.

8. I don't want to complain because they cleaned the apartment for me.

9. We secretaries deserve a raise.

10. He bought her some flowers, but he didn't give them to her.

# Leísmo, Loísmo, and Laísmo

Given the fact that the direct object, indirect object, and reflexive pronouns are the same in the first and second persons, it might be expected that there would be some variation in usage with the only case where these differ. In fact, there is a fair amount of variation in the Spanish-speaking world with regard to the use of third-person singular and plural direct object and indirect object pronouns.

The pronoun system shown below in which **lo, la, los, las** are used as direct object pronouns and **le** and **les** are reserved for indirect objects is typical of Latin American Spanish. This system of object pronoun usage is known as **loísmo**. Because it clearly distinguishes direct objects from indirect objects, **loísmo** is perhaps the simplest system to learn.

Nevertheless, it is understandable that speakers might want to distinguish direct objects that refer to people from those that do not. This desire to mark a distinction between human and nonhuman direct objects explains the existence of a second system of pronoun usage called **leísmo**. With **leísmo** the pronouns **le** and **les** are used for indirect objects, both masculine and feminine, as well as for masculine singular direct objects. Note that with **loísmo** and **leísmo**, the feminine direct object pronouns would be **la** and **las**. Both **loísmo** and **leísmo** are accepted by the Real Academia, with **loísmo** being the general rule in Latin America and **leísmo** being more common in Spain. It should be pointed out that there is some confusion with regard to the term **loísmo**. Some use the term to refer to a nonstandard usage of the pronoun **lo** as an indirect object pronoun. However, this is not the way the term **loísmo** is used by most Spanish grammarians.

A third system of pronoun usage which is not accepted by the Real Academia is the use of the direct object pronoun for indirect objects that refer to human females. Although condemned by many, **laísmo** is fairly common in some parts of Spain. The following table and examples illustrate the differences in these three pronoun systems.

| | | |
|---|---|---|
| Lo conocí anoche. | *I met him last night.* | |
| Le di un regalo (a él). | *I gave him a gift.* | **(loísmo)** |
| La vi en la tienda. | *I saw her at the store.* | |
| Le mandé una carta (a ella). | *I sent her a letter.* | |
| | | |
| Le conocí anoche. | *I met him last night.* | |
| Le di un regalo (a él). | *I gave him a gift.* | **(leísmo)** |
| La vi en la tienda. | *I saw her at the store.* | |
| Le mandé una carta (a ella) | *I sent her a letter.* | |
| | | |
| Le conocí anoche. | *I met him last night.* | |
| Le di un regalo (a él). | *I gave him a gift.* | **(laísmo)** |
| La vi en la tienda. | *I saw her at the store.* | |
| La mandé una carta (a ella). | *I sent her a letter.* | |

### Leísmo, Loísmo, and Laísmo

**Loísmo**

| Direct Object Pronouns | | Indirect Object Pronouns | |
|---|---|---|---|
| me | nos | me | nos |
| te | os | te | os |
| lo, la | los, las | le | les |

**Leísmo**

| Direct Object Pronouns | | Indirect Object Pronouns | |
|---|---|---|---|
| me | nos | me | nos |
| te | os | te | os |
| le, la | los, las | le | les |

**Laísmo**

| Direct Object Pronouns | | Indirect Object Pronouns | |
|---|---|---|---|
| me | nos | me | nos |
| te | os | te | os |
| le, la | los, las | le, la | les |

## Demonstrative Pronouns and Adjectives

For the sake of convenience, both demonstrative pronouns and adjectives will be discussed here. Demonstrative pronouns take the place of a noun and indicate its location in time or space in relation to the speaker and listener. In the chart below, one can see the parallel relationship between these forms and the adverbs **aquí**, **ahí**, and **allí** which also denote location. Demonstrative pronouns, with the exception of the neuters, carry an accent. The demonstrative adjectives have the same forms as the demonstrative pronouns, but they modify rather than replace the nouns. Demonstrative adjectives carry no accent and generally precede the nouns they modify.

Esta silla es más cómoda que ésa.
*This chair is more comfortable than that one (near you).*

¿Te gusta este carro?
*Do you like this car (here)?*

No, prefiero aquél.
*No, I prefer that one (over there).*

Recuerdo aquellos días de mi juventud.
*I remember those days of my youth.*

| Demonstrative Adjectives and Pronouns | | | |
|---|---|---|---|
| | Demonstrative Pronoun | Demonstrative Adjective | Adverb |
| Near the speaker | éste<br>ésta<br>éstos<br>éstas | este<br>esta<br>estos<br>estas | aquí (acá) |
| Near the listener | ése<br>ésa<br>ésos<br>ésas | ese<br>esa<br>esos<br>esas | ahí |
| Far from both | aquél<br>aquélla<br>aquéllos<br>aquéllas | aquel<br>aquella<br>aquellos<br>aquellas | allí (allá) |

Spanish also has three neuter demonstrative pronouns: **esto**, **eso**, and **aquello**. These are used to refer to unspecified objects or to abstract ideas, actions or situations. They never carry a written accent and can never be used as adjectives; thus, they never precede a noun.

Esto es interesante.　　　　　　　　*This is interesting.*
No debo mencionar eso.　　　　　　*I should not mention that.*
Eso no puede ser.　　　　　　　　　*That can't be.*

**Exercise 5.** Fill in the blank with the correct demonstrative adjective or pronoun.

1. Yo no quiero comprar_____pulsera aquí; prefiero_____que tienes tú.

2. No puedo creer que dijiste_____.

3. En_____época no había muchos edificios aquí.

4. Quiero probarme_____vestido que tengo o_____que está cerca de usted.

5. Yo veo que bebes algo, hijo. ¿Quién te trajo_____botella de cerveza?

6. No sé qué es_____que tengo en la mano.

7. _____no son las mismas mentiras que me dijiste ayer.

8. Todavía me acuerdo de la belleza de _____chicas venezolanas.

# Reflexives and Other Uses of Se

| Reflexive Pronouns | |
|---|---|
| me | nos |
| te | os |
| se | se |

Reflexive pronouns are used in both English and Spanish to indicate that the direct or indirect object of a sentence has the same referent as the subject. In other words, the subject of the sentence is both the doer and the receiver of the action. The action performed is thus "reflected" back on the subject. In English the reflexive pronouns end with –*self* or -*selves*. In Spanish the reflexive pronouns are distinguished from direct and indirect object pronouns only in the third-person singular and plural forms. There is a great deal of variation in the way reflexives are currently treated in Spanish grammar textbooks. Some authors treat the reflexive as having a single usage, while others divide reflexives into several different categories. Six categories were chosen here to clarify reflexive usage.

## "True" Reflexive Se

Many verbs can be used reflexively in Spanish. In the examples below, the reflexive and nonreflexive uses of some verbs are contrasted. Sentences such as the first in each pair of examples below are often described as being "true" or "literal" uses of the reflexive. In these cases, because the entity performing the action is the same one who receives the action, a reflexive pronoun is used. When the subject is performing the action on someone else, the sentence is not reflexive, and a reflexive pronoun is not used. Verbs which are often used in a "true" reflexive sense include **acostarse**, **afeitarse**, **cepillarse**, **ducharse**, **lavarse**, **limpiarse**, **peinarse**, **quemarse**, **romperse**, and **vestirse**.

| | | |
|---|---|---|
| Ana se bañó. | *Ana took a bath.* | (reflexive) |
| Ana bañó su perro. | *Ana bathed her dog.* | (nonreflexive) |
| | | |
| Me lavé la cabeza. | *I washed my hair.* | (reflexive) |
| Yo lavé el coche. | *I washed the car.* | (nonreflexive) |
| | | |
| Nos acostamos a las nueve. | *We go to bed at nine.* | (reflexive) |
| Acostamos a nuestro hijo a las nueve. | *We put our son to bed at nine.* | (nonreflexive) |

### Inherent Se

There are some verbs which use the reflexive pronoun without any apparent grammatical reason. These must simply be memorized as requiring the reflexive pronoun. In some cases, it is clear that the subject is not the receiver of the action. Instead, the reflexive pronoun is somehow considered to be "inherent" to the meaning of the verb. In the examples below, it is very clear that these individuals did not complain to or inform themselves.

| | |
|---|---|
| Él se quejaba de todo. | *He complained about everything.* |
| Ella se fugó. | *She ran away.* |
| Se atrevió a entrar con esa chica. | *He dared to come in with that girl.* |
| Me enteré de la situación. | *I found out about the situation.* |

With some verbs, the use of a reflexive pronoun will change the meaning of the verb. Some common examples of these are included in the table below.

| Meaning-Changing Reflexive Verbs | | | |
|---|---|---|---|
| acordar | *to agree* | acordarse | *to remember* |
| dormir | *to sleep* | dormirse | *to fall asleep* |
| ir | *to go* | irse | *to go away* |
| llegar | *to arrive* | llegarse | *to approach* |
| levantar | *to lift, raise* | levantarse | *to get up, stand up* |
| marchar | *to march* | marcharse | *to leave, go away* |
| poner | *to put, place* | ponerse | *to put on clothes, to become* |
| parecer | *to seem, appear* | parecerse | *to resemble, look like* |
| volver | *to return* | volverse | *to turn around, to become* |

### Reciprocal Se

When the pronouns **se**, **os** or **nos** are used in sense of *each other*, or *one another*, they are called reciprocal constructions.

| | |
|---|---|
| Se ven todos los días. | *They see each other every day.* |
| Nos queremos mucho. | *We love each other very much.* |
| Se conocieron el año pasado. | *They met (each other) last year.* |

### Impersonal/Passive Se

The impersonal/passive **se** is used in sentences where there is no specific referent for the subject of the sentence. Some authors make a grammatical distinction between the impersonal **se** and the passive **se**. However, because the two are so similar in meaning, they are often considered as one category and will be treated as such here.

In many cases, the impersonal/passive **se** corresponds to the English impersonal expressions such as *you, they, people, one, we,* or as a substitute for the true Spanish passive construction **ser + past participle**.

| | | |
|---|---|---|
| ¿Cómo se dice eso en español? | *How does one say that in Spanish?* | |
| No se juega fútbol en la casa. | *We don't play soccer in the house.* | |
| Se prohíbe fumar | *Smoking is prohibted.* | |
| | | |
| Se rompieron los vasos. | *The glasses were broken.* | (more common) |
| Los vasos fueron rotos. | | (less common) |
| Se vendió el carro. | *The car was sold.* | (more common) |
| El carro fue vendido. | | (less common) |

It is helpful to make a distinction between the use of the passive/impersonal **se** with inanimate objects and its use with human beings. When the passive/impersonal **se** is used with inanimate objects, these function as the subject of the sentence. For this reason, the verb will agree in number with the inanimate objects. When **se** is used with intransitive verbs, the third-person singular form is always used.

| | |
|---|---|
| Se venden carros aquí. | *Cars are sold here.* |
| Aquí se habla español. | *Spanish is spoken here.* |
| Se vive bien aquí. | *We live well here.* |

## Se of Unplanned Occurrence

One very common use of the pronoun **se** in Spanish which sometimes strikes English speakers as unusual is its use in so-called "accidental" or "unplanned" occurrences. Such events may include dropping, breaking, forgetting, etc. In these constructions the verb agrees in number with the subject of the sentence, which is the thing being dropped, lost, etc. In these cases, the subject generally comes at the end of the sentence. The indirect object pronoun is used to refer to the person who experienced the unplanned occurrence. If one wishes to refer more specifically to the person who experiences the event, a phrase introduced by the preposition **a** is used.

| | |
|---|---|
| Se me rompió el reloj. | *I broke my watch.* |
| Se le perdieron los zapatos. | *He lost his shoes.* |
| Se le olvidó la llave a Juan. | *Juan forgot his key.* |

## Se of Completion or Totality

The reflexive pronoun can also be used with some verbs to emphasize or highlight the completeness or totality of an action.

| | |
|---|---|
| Comí la pizza. | *I ate the pizza.* |
| Me comí la pizza | *I ate up the whole pizza.* |
| | |
| Aprendí la lección anoche. | *I learned the lesson last night.* |
| Me aprendí la lección en una noche. | *I learned the whole lesson in one night.* |
| | |
| Bébelo. | *Drink it.* |
| Bébetelo. | *Drink it all up (or down).* |

## The Neuter Pronoun Lo

The neuter pronoun **lo** is used when a speaker wishes to refer back to a concept, an idea, or a situation.

| | |
|---|---|
| Ella fue a la fiesta. | *She went to the party.* |
| Sí, lo sé. | *Yes, I know (that she went).* |
| | |
| Ellos van a ofrecerle el trabajo. | *They are going to offer him the job.* |
| No lo creo. | *I don't believe it.* |
| | |
| Juan se casó anoche. | *Juan got married last night.* |
| ¿Verdad? No lo sabía. | *Really? I didn't know.* |

The neuter pronoun is used to replace predicate nominatives or predicate adjectives.

| | |
|---|---|
| ¿Es inteligente tu novia? | *Is your girlfriend smart?* |
| Sí, lo es. | *Yes, she is.* |
| | |
| ¿Están enfermos? | *Are they sick?* |
| No, no lo están. | *No, they are not.* |

## Lexical Differences

### SABER/CONOCER/PODER

**Saber**-*to know facts, information, or how to do something*

This verb is used for *to know* in the sense having learned something by memorizing it or studying it. **Saber** is also used with infinitives in the sense of knowing how to do something.

| | |
|---|---|
| Ella sabe la verdad. | *She knows the truth.* |
| Yo sé la fecha de tu nacimiento. | *I know your birth date.* |
| Juan sabe el poema; lo estudió mucho. | *Juan knows the poem. He studied it a lot.* |

**Conocer**-*to know or be familiar with*

**Conocer** is used for knowing in the sense of being acquainted with or familiar with a person. It is used less frequently to talk about being familiar with a thing or a place. In the preterit tense, it is used to mean *to meet someone* for the first time.

| | |
|---|---|
| Conozco a María. | *I know María.* |
| Ellos no conocen a esa señorita. | *They don't know that woman.* |
| Nos conocimos en la fiesta. | *We met at the party.* |
| No conoce Miami. | *He is not familiar with Miami.* |
| Conozco esa canción. | *I know that song. (I have heard it.)* |

**Poder**-*can, to be able to*

The verb **poder** is often used where English uses the modal *can*. It can be used for asking or giving permission, or it can be used with infinitives to express that one is physically able to do something. However, knowing how to do something is expressed by **saber** rather than **poder**.

| | |
|---|---|
| No puedo hablar contigo ahora. | *I can't speak with you now.* |
| Ellos no pueden ir esta noche. | *They can't go tonight.* |
| Me duele la pierna; no puedo caminar. | *My leg hurts; I can't walk.* |
| Mi mamá dice que no puedo nadar hoy. | *My mom says I can't swim today.* |
| Yo no sé nadar. | *I can't (don't know how to) swim.* |
| Ella sabe cocinar muy bien. | *She can (knows how to) cook very well.* |

**Exercise 6.** Translate the following sentences to Spanish.

1. They are going to turn in the homework before leaving.

2. I tried to help him, but he bit me.

3. He can't read, but that doesn't mean he isn't intelligent.

4. They buy textbooks here.

5. I need this notebook, but you can return it to me tomorrow.

6. Don't tell him about the job if you are not going to offer it to him.

7. I think I broke my leg, but I can walk.

8. She met him on Friday and asked him for his telephone number.

9. You need to ask them if they plan to support you.

10. They love each other very much.

11. I swear to you that there is no more cake. Marcos ate it all up.
_____

12. He lost his watch, so he arrived late for the interview.
_____

13. They eat well in Louisiana.
_____

14. I always feel better when I get up early.
_____

15. He got up and turned on the television.
_____

# CHAPTER 4

# Preterit and Imperfect

## Preterit Tense

**Regular Preterit Conjugations**

Regular **-ar** verbs are conjugated in the preterit by adding **-é, -aste, -ó, -amos, -asteis,** and **-aron** to the stem. The conjugation endings for both **-er** and **-ir** verbs in the preterit are: **-í, -iste, -ió, -imos, -isteis** and **-ieron**.

| Preterit Conjugations: Regular –AR, -ER, and –IR VERBS | | |
|---|---|---|
| **-AR** | **-ER** | **-IR** |
| **Hablar** | **Comer** | **Vivir** |
| hablé | comí | viví |
| hablaste | comiste | viviste |
| habló | comió | vivió |
| hablamos | comimos | vivimos |
| hablasteis | comisteis | vivisteis |
| hablaron | comieron | vivieron |

**Spelling-Change Preterit Verbs**

Verbs that end in **-car, -gar** and **-zar** will have a change in the first-person singular only. With another set of **-er** and **-ir** verbs, the **-i-** of the **-ió** and **-ieron** endings of the third-person singular and plural forms becomes **-y-**.

| Preterit Tense Conjugations : I to Y Spelling-Change Verbs | | | |
|---|---|---|---|
| **Leer** | **Caer** | **Oír** | **Creer** |
| leí | caí | oí | creí |
| leíste | caíste | oíste | creíste |
| leyó | cayó | oyó | creyó |
| leímos | caímos | oímos | creímos |
| leísteis | caísteis | oísteis | creísteis |
| leyeron | cayeron | oyeron | creyeron |

| Preterit Tense Conjugations: -GAR, -CAR, and –ZAR Spelling-Change Verbs | | |
|---|---|---|
| c to qu | g to gu | z to c |
| **Buscar** | **Pagar** | **Almorzar** |
| busqué | pagué | almorcé |
| buscaste | pagaste | almorzaste |
| buscó | pagó | almorzó |
| buscamos | pagamos | almorzamos |
| buscasteis | pagasteis | almorzasteis |
| buscaron | pagaron | almorzaron |
| Other **c to qu** verbs | Other **g to gu** verbs | Other **z to c** verbs |
| explicar | apagar | alcanzar |
| indicar | colgar | comenzar |
| sacar | jugar | cruzar |
| tocar | llegar | empezar |

**Exercise 1.** Conjugate the following verbs in the preterit.

1. ellos (to write) _____
2. nosotros (to live) _____
3. ella (to escape) _____
4. yo (to look for) _____
5. usted (to drink) _____
6. ella (to begin) _____
7. yo (to play) _____
8. mis padres (to turn off) _____
9. mi prima (to hear) _____
10. ellos (to ask) _____
11. Juan (to earn) _____
12. ustedes (to return) _____
13. yo (to arrive) _____
14. nosotros (to learn) _____
15. Ana y Marcos (to read) _____
16. tú (to eat) _____
17. ella (to fall) _____
18. usted (to cross) _____
19. tú (to take out) _____
20. yo (to send) _____

## Stem-Changing Preterit Verbs

The three types of stem-changing verbs in the present tense, **e to ie**, **o to ue**, and **e to i**, are collapsed into only two types in the preterit: **e to i** and **o to u**. No **-ar** or **-er** verbs have a stem change in the preterit. All **-ir** verbs which have stem changes in the present tense will have a stem change in the preterit. In the preterit, however, these changes occur only in the third-person singular and third-person plural forms of **-ir** verbs.

| Preterit Tense Conjugations: -IR Stem-Changing Verbs | |
|---|---|
| e to i | o to u |
| **Pedir** | **Dormir** |
| pedí | dormí |
| pediste | dormiste |
| pidió | durmió |
| pedimos | dormimos |
| pedisteis | dormisteis |
| pidieron | durmieron |

## Preterit Verbs with an Irregular Stem

A number of verbs have an irregularity in both the stem and the conjugation endings. The easiest way to learn these verbs is to learn a third set of preterit endings and the stem for each verb. The third-person singular form of the verb **hacer** is **hizo**. The verbs whose stems end in **-j-** will drop the **-i-** in the third-person plural forms: **dijeron**, **trajeron**, etc.

| Stems and Endings for Irregular-Stem Verbs | | |
|---|---|---|
| **Verb** | **Stem** | **Endings** |
| tener | tuv | |
| estar | estuv | |
| venir | vin | e |
| saber | sup | iste |
| poner | pus | o |
| poder | pud | imos |
| andar | anduv | isteis |
| caber | cup | ieron |
| hacer | hic (hizo) | |
| traer | traj (trajeron) | |
| decir | dij (dijeron) | |

### Preterit Tense Conjugations: Irregular-Stem Preterit Verbs

| **Tener** | **Estar** | **Saber** | **Poner** | **Poder** |
|---|---|---|---|---|
| tuve | estuve | supe | puse | pude |
| tuviste | estuviste | supiste | pusiste | pudiste |
| tuvo | estuvo | supo | puso | pudo |
| tuvimos | estuvimos | supimos | pusimos | pudimos |
| tuvisteis | estuvisteis | supisteis | pusisteis | pudisteis |
| tuvieron | estuvieron | supieron | pusieron | pudieron |

| **Andar** | **Caber** | **Hacer** | **Traer** | **Decir** |
|---|---|---|---|---|
| anduve | cupe | hice | traje | dije |
| anduviste | cupiste | hiciste | trajiste | dijiste |
| anduvo | cupo | hizo | trajo | dijo |
| anduvimos | cupimos | hicimos | trajimos | dijimos |
| anduvisteis | cupisteis | hicisteis | trajisteis | dijisteis |
| anduvieron | cupieron | hicieron | trajeron | dijeron |

Some verbs are completely irregular in the preterit tense and must be memorized. The verbs **ser** and **ir** have the same conjugation in the preterit.

### Preterit Tense Conjugations: Other Irregular Verbs

| **Ser** | **Ir** | **Dar** |
|---|---|---|
| fui | fui | di |
| fuiste | fuiste | diste |
| fue | fue | dio |
| fuimos | fuimos | dimos |
| fuisteis | fuisteis | disteis |
| fueron | fueron | dieron |

**Exercise 2.** Fill in the blank with the correct preterit form.

1. ellos (to sleep)_____
2. yo (to go) _____
3. tú (to ask for, order) _____
4. ellos (to serve) _____
5. nosotros (to give) _____
6. Juan (to eat) _____

7. ella (to die) _____
8. Marta (to be) _____
9. yo (to lie) _____
10. usted (to drink) _____
11. ustedes (to have) _____
12. tu abuelo (to do, make) _____
13. yo (to arrive) _____
14. nuestro tío (to bring) _____
15. mi hermano (to drink) _____
16. los chicos (to walk) _____
17. tú (to find out) _____
18. usted (to follow) _____
19. la profesora (to read) _____
20. ellos (to say, tell) _____

**Exercise 3.** Translate the following sentences to Spanish.

1. When did you leave your house this morning?

2. Did you work last night?

3. No, I stayed home and watched TV.

4. What did you do last night?

5. I went to the movies with Marta.

6. Later we went to a restaurant to eat.

7. After eating, I paid the bill and we left.

8. Did you give her the necklace that you bought her last week?

9. No, I am going to give it to her tomorrow.

10. I am going to take a bath and go to bed.

11. Where did you put the towels?
___

12. I don't know. Marcos didn't give them to you?
___

13. No, I looked for them this morning, but I didn't find them.
___

14. He forgot to take them out of the washer again.
___

15. I love life in the dorm.
___

## Imperfect Tense

**Imperfect Tense Conjugations: Regular Verbs**

| **Hablar** | **Comer** | **Vivir** |
|---|---|---|
| hablaba | comía | vivía |
| hablabas | comías | vivías |
| hablaba | comía | vivía |
| hablábamos | comíamos | vivíamos |
| hablabais | comíais | vivíais |
| hablaban | comían | vivían |

Regular **-ar** verbs are conjugated in the imperfect tense by adding **-aba, -abas, -aba, -ábamos, -abais,** and **-aban** to their stems. The endings for regular **-er** and **-ir** verbs are **-ía, -ías, -ía, -íamos, -íais,** and **ían**. There are only three verbs that are irregular in the imperfect tense.

**Imperfect Conjugations: Irregular Verbs**

| **Ser** | **Ir** | **Ver** |
|---|---|---|
| era | iba | veía |
| eras | ibas | veías |
| era | iba | veía |
| éramos | íbamos | veíamos |
| erais | ibais | veíais |
| eran | iban | veían |

**Exercise 4.** Conjugate the following verbs in the imperfect tense.

1. ellos (to walk)_____
2. Juan y María (to see) _____
3. yo (to be) _____
4. nosotros (to play) _____
5. el profesor (to help) _____

6. tú (to go) _____
7. nuestro tío (to give) _____
8. usted (to put, place) _____
9. mis amigos (to come) _____
10. la mamá de Ana (to cry) _____

## Use of Preterit and Imperfect

For many students, the distinction between the preterit and the imperfect is one of the most problematic areas of Spanish grammar. In discussing the differences between the preterit and the imperfect, it is helpful to distinguish the meaning of the terms *tense* and *aspect*. The term *tense* indicates the time at which an action occurs in the past, present, or future. Aspect characterizes a past, present, or future action as being initiative, continuous, or terminative.

For many English-speaking students, the major difficulty with the preterit and imperfect arises from the fact that English has only one simple past tense while Spanish has both the preterit and the imperfect. Although the preterit and imperfect are generally referred to as two different tenses, both are actually past tenses. The difference between the two is really one of aspect; they are used to describe past actions in different ways.

Whether a speaker uses the preterit or imperfect will depend upon how he or she wishes to characterize a particular action. The preterit tense is used to describe the beginning point of an action, the ending point of an action, or to show that an action or event has been completed. The imperfect tense is used to characterize actions as being continuous or repeated in the past. While English does sometimes show aspectual differences in the past, this is most often done through use of adverbial expressions rather than by marking the verb in some way. Thus, the aspectual information is not always apparent in the English verb forms themselves.

| | |
|---|---|
| We prepared dinner last night, and he **ate** with us. | (perfective) |
| As he **ate**, he told us about the accident. | (imperfective) |
| When he was young, he **ate** there every day. | (imperfective) |

In the first sentence above, the action is viewed as having been completed. The second sentence highlights the mid-point of the action; the eating is taking place without reference to the beginning or ending of the action. The third sentence suggests customary or repeated action in the past. Very often either the preterit or imperfect may be used in the same sentence structure with different meanings.

Ella gritó cuando él entró. (perfective, perfective)
*She screamed when he came in.*

Ella gritaba cuando él entró. (imperfective, perfective)
*She was screaming when he came in.*

Ella gritaba cuando él entraba. (imperfective, imperfective)
*She was screaming as he was coming in.*

Ella gritó cuando él entraba. (perfective, imperfective)
*She screamed as he was coming in.*

    Generally speaking, action verbs such as **caminar**, **golpear**, **correr**, and **romper** are used more often in the preterit tense. Stative verbs such as **ser**, **estar**, **poder**, and **querer** are used more frequently in the imperfect tense. However, the following discussion will highlight the fact that either preterit or imperfect can be used with any verb; the tense is determined by the intended meaning of the speaker.

    In Spanish or in English an event can be viewed in terms of its beginning point (initiative), its ending point (terminative), or as an event which has been completed. These events are said to be perfective in aspect. In Spanish the preterit is used to signal perfective aspect regardless of how long the event may have lasted.

De repente la chica corrió hacia los caballos. (initiative)
*Suddenly the girl took off running towards the horses.*

Los chicos dejaron de hablar. (terminative)
*The boys stopped talking.*

Llovió por cuarenta días. (completed event)
*It rained for forty days.*

    On the other hand, the same actions could be viewed as an ongoing or repeated past actions. The imperfect tense is used in Spanish to convey these imperfective past actions. In contrast to the preterit, the imperfect gives no indication of the beginning or ending point of an action. Instead, the imperfect brings the reader or listener into the middle of the action with no reference to its beginning or ending. It might be said that the imperfect provides background or "sets the stage" for the main actions or events (in the preterit) that move the story or conversation forward.

Ellos comían cuando sonó el teléfono. (ongoing, perfective)
*They were eating when the telephone rang.*

Mientras yo trabajaba, mi hija hacía su tarea. (ongoing, imperfective)
*While I was working, my daughter was doing her homework.*

Yo jugaba fútbol todos los días cuando era niño. (repeated, imperfective)
*I used to play soccer every day when I was a child.*

En los veranos, siempre nadábamos en el río. (repeated, imperfective)
*In the summers, we always swam in the river.*

## Imperfect with States or Conditions

Some verbs describe states or conditions which by their very nature seem to indicate continuing or ongoing action. The imperfect tense is used more than the preterit with these verbs that express emotional, physical, or mental conditions in the past. The preterit may be used with these verbs if one wishes to highlight the point at which the condition began, to limit the period of its duration, or to indicate a change in condition.

Yo tenía dolor de cabeza y estaba mareado.
*I had a headache and I was dizzy.*

Me dolió la cabeza toda la noche.
*My head hurt all night.*

Me alegraba porque mi sobrina estaba conmigo.
*I was happy because my niece was with me.*

Al ver a mi sobrina, me alegré.
*I became very happy when I saw my niece.*

Estaba en la fiesta cuando la llamaste.
*She was at the party when you called her.*

Estuvo en la fiesta por tres horas.
*She was at the party for three hours.*

Some other verbs relating to knowledge, desire, possession, or perception present special problems as they seem to "change meanings" depending upon whether the preterit or imperfect tense is used. Because of the meanings of these verbs, they are often thought of as being inherently imperfective. Thus, when the preterit tense is used with these verbs in Spanish, the initiative or terminative action rather than the process itself is emphasized.

| | |
|---|---|
| La conocí anoche.<br>*I met her last night.* | (completed action) |
| La conocía bien.<br>*I knew her well.* | (continuing state) |
| Tuve que estudiar anoche.<br>*I had to study last night (and I did).* | (completed action) |
| Tenía que estudiar anoche.<br>*I had to study last night (but I may or may not have done so).* | (continuing state) |
| El libro costó veinte dólares.<br>*The book cost twenty dollars (and I bought it).* | (completed action) |

El libro costaba veinte dólares  (continuing state)
*The price of the book was five dollars.*

En 2005 la mujer tuvo dos hijos.  (completed action)
*In 2005 the woman gave birth to two children.*

En 2005 la mujer tenía dos hijos.  (continuing state)
*In 2005 the woman was the mother of two children.*

El chico no quiso cantar.  (completed action)
*The boy refused to sing.*

El chico no quería cantar.  (continuing state)
*The boy did not want to sing (but he may have done so).*

El día de la boda yo supe que ella no me quería.  (completed action)
*The day of the wedding I found out the she did not love me.*

El día de la boda yo sabía que ella no me quería.  (continuing state)
*The day of the wedding I already knew she didn't love me.*

No pude caminar.  (completed action)
*I tried to walk (and failed).*

No podía caminar.  (continuing state)
*I did not have the ability to walk (may or may not have tried).*

**Exercise 5.** Translate the following sentences to Spanish.

1. My friend María called me at 9:00 last night.

2. I was reading when the phone rang.

3. When I answered the phone, María said that she needed to talk to someone.

4. María told me that her mother was sick and that she was afraid.

5. She said her mother used to smoke every day when she was young.

6. María said her mother had to go to the hospital the next day.

7. The doctor said that he was going to do some tests.

8. We talked for two hours.

9. I wanted to talk more, but I had to hang up because Juan came to the door.

10. He said that he had some problems that he wanted to discuss.

11. When John finally left an hour later, I was very sleepy.

12. I took a shower and went to bed.

**Exercise 6.** Translate the following to Spanish.

1. They found out that he had erased the signature.

2. I refused to go with them because they were drunk.

3. We were at the party for two hours.

4. I knew the man who had left us the food.

5. He told us three times that we needed more money.

6. While we were sleeping, someone knocked at the door.

7. I told them that I was going to faint.

8. The woman that helped us was very tall.

9. We knew that we had an exam the next day, but we decided to go out.

10. I wasn't able to go because my mom was mad at me. Did you have fun?

**Exercise 7.** Translate the following paragraph to Spanish.

Last Saturday night my parents went to a party at my aunt's house. I decided to stay home because I wasn't feeling well, and I knew that I was going to have a test on Monday. While I was studying in my room, I heard something strange. I got up and went to the window, but I didn't see anything. Everything seemed completely normal. Suddenly, I heard the noise again. I realized that it was inside the house. I was really scared. I grabbed my umbrella, opened the door of my room, and walked into the hallway. I was walking towards my parents' room when I heard a strange voice. Someone was saying my name: "Maya . . . . Maya". I realized that the voice was coming from the closet in my parents' room. I went into the room, walked over to the closet, lifted up the umbrella, and opened to closet door. Inside the closet I discovered my cat Susana. She was underneath a pile of clothes. She ran out of the closet, and I almost fell down. The next time my aunt gives a party, I am not going to stay home.

**Exercise 8.** Fill in the blank with either the preterit or imperfect tense.

La Cita de Juan y María

Juan y yo nos divertimos mucho anoche. Juan (1. estar) estudiando para un examen de química y yo (2. mirar) la televisión. A las siete yo (3. entrar) en el cuarto y le (4. preguntar) a Juan si (5. querer) ir al cine conmigo. Juan me (6. decir) que sí porque (7. sentirse) un poco cansado. Nosotros (8. salir) inmediatamente para el cine. (9. Ver) una película romántica. Después, nosotros (10. ir) a nuestro café favorito. Como (11. hacer) frío, (12. tomar) café con leche y (13. hablar) por como dos horas. (14. Ser) la una de la mañana cuando (15. regresar) a casa. Yo (16. acostarse) porque (17. estar) muy cansada. Juan (18. tener) sueño, pero (19. empezar) a estudiar otra vez porque (20. saber) que el examen lo esperaba.

1._____ 2._____ 3._____

4._____ 5._____ 6._____

7._____ 8._____ 9._____

10._____ 11._____ 12._____

13._____ 14._____ 15._____

16._____ 17._____ 18._____

19._____ 20._____

## Lexical Differences

### POR/PORQUE/A CAUSA DE/COMO

**Por; A causa de**-*because of*

Because **por** is a preposition, it can be used before nouns or some pronouns in the sense of *because of*. The preposition **a causa de** is used in the same way as **por** in the sense of *on account of* or *because of*.

**Porque**-*because*

The conjunction **porque** joins two clauses. The construction *\*porque de* does not exist in Spanish.

| | |
|---|---|
| Yo llegué tarde por el tráfico. | *I arrived late because of the traffic.* |
| Lo hicimos por él. | *We did it for him.* |
| Ella no fue a causa del accidente. | *She did not go because of the accident.* |
| Saliste mal porque no estudiaste. | *You did poorly because you didn't study.* |

**Como**-*because*

**Como** is most often used at the beginning of a sentence where English would use the expressions *because* or *since*.

Como teníamos mucho trabajo, no salimos.
*Since we had a lot of work, we didn't go out.*

Como ya era muy tarde, decidieron quedarse en casa.
*Since it was already late, they decided to stay home.*

## TIEMPO/ÉPOCA/VEZ/HORA

When one is speaking of time in a general sense, as a block of time, or a period of time, the noun **tiempo** is used.

| | |
|---|---|
| No tenemos mucho tiempo. | *We don't have much time.* |
| Yo pasé mucho tiempo en Madrid. | *I spent a lot of time in Madrid.* |

**Tiempo** can also be used to mean *weather*.

| | |
|---|---|
| ¿Qué tiempo hace hoy? | *What is the weather like today?* |
| Hace mal tiempo. | *The weather is bad.* |

**Época**-*time; period*

For reference to a longer period of time or one that is farther removed from the present time, the noun **época** may be used.

| | |
|---|---|
| En esa época viajábamos en tren. | *In those days, we used to travel by train.* |
| Durante aquella época no había aviones. | *During that time, there were no airplanes.* |

**Vez**-*occurrence; occasion*

The noun **vez** is used for time in the sense of one or more occurences.

| | |
|---|---|
| Hablamos con ella tres veces. | *We spoke with her three times.* |
| Voy a llamarla otra vez. | *I am going to call her again.* |
| Esta vez yo voy a hacerlo. | *This time I am going to do it.* |
| Muchas veces nos quedamos en casa. | *Many times (often) we stay home.* |

**Hora**-*time, hour*

When talking about the time of day or what time an event will occur, **hora** is used.

| | |
|---|---|
| ¿Qué hora es? | *What time is it?* |
| Es hora de salir. | *It is time to go out.* |

**Exercise 9.** Translate the following sentences to Spanish.

1. At that time there were no roads in these woods.
___

2. She wanted to spend more time with her children.
___

3. She left early because of the rain.
___

4. She was a teacher for three years.
___

5. Because I don't have to work today, we can go to the movies.
___

6. We were happy because we saw that he was fine.
___

7. One time we went to their house to swim.
___

8. He said that the weather was nice, but we decided to stay home.
___

9. It rained for eight days, but we were finally able to finish the building.
___

10. He retired last year because he wanted to travel.
___

# CHAPTER 5

# Ser and Estar

## Difficulties With *to be* in Spanish

Knowing how to express the English verb *to be* in Spanish can be challenging for students. This fact should not be surprising given the number of ways *to be* can be translated in Spanish.

| | |
|---|---|
| Juan es profesor. | *Juan is a professor.* |
| Ana está enferma. | *Ana is sick.* |
| Ellos tienen miedo. | *They are afraid.* |
| Yo preparo la comida. | *I am preparing the food.* |
| Hay tres ventanas en la clase. | *There are three windows in the class.* |
| Hace frío hoy. | *It is cold today.* |

The verbs **ser** and **estar** can be especially troublesome for students. In some cases two sentences in Spanish may be identical except for the verb **ser** or **estar**. Often these sentences may even be translated in the same way in English. However, the choice of **ser** or **estar** will change the meaning of the sentence in Spanish.

| | |
|---|---|
| Ella es nerviosa. | *She is a nervous person.* |
| Ella está nerviosa. | *She is nervous (right now).* |

Because of the difficulty associated with distinguishing between the verbs **ser** and **estar**, many elementary Spanish texts begin by providing lists of uses of both verbs. While the use of such lists seems to be the simplest way to help elementary students begin to grasp the basic distinction between **ser** and **estar**, there are some problems associated with their use.

For example, the student who glances at a list may draw incorrect conclusions about the relative frequency of the use of the two verbs. The more serious problem, however, stems from the fact that lists are often misinterpreted. For example, by simply looking at the list, students sometimes conclude that **gordo** '*fat*', and **joven** '*young*', are "physical conditions" and are then confused about why they are most often used with the verb **ser**.

Lists can be very helpful when used as a reference point. In fact, a list will be provided for this purpose at the end of this section. However, such lists are most effective when accompanied by an in-depth explanation of the difference in the basic nature of these two verbs. The goal here is to move students away from reliance on the list and more in the direction of a native-like intuition about the basic difference between the two verbs.

## Uses of the Verb Ser

The verb **ser** is used to describe the basic nature or essence of a person or thing; it is used to refer to an inherent characteristic of the subject. When used with an adjective, the verb **ser** can be thought of as basically equating the subject with the adjective used. **Ser** is used to make general or objective statements about the basic or essential characteristics of a person or thing.

These so-called "usual characteristics" are considered to be relatively stable and not as subject to change. However, it is sometimes difficult to determine whether a given characteristic can be considered basic, essential, or inherent. For that matter, there is no concrete way to distinguish between what is stable and what is transitory. Perhaps the most helpful way to think about the verb **ser** is that it describes someone or something within the framework of what is normal or usual for the entity in question.

**Ser** is used with adjectives to describe usual or inherent characteristics, origin, nationality, religion, profession, size, shape, color, etc. In these cases, the verb **ser** is often said to function as a sort of equal sign joining the two sentence elements.

| | |
|---|---|
| María es mexicana. | *María is Mexican.* |
| Juan es abogado. | *Juan is a lawyer.* |
| María y Juan son católicos. | *Mary and John are Catholic.* |
| La casa es grande. | *The house is large.* |

**Ser** is used with expressions relating to time, dates, days of the week, and seasons.

| | |
|---|---|
| La clase comienza a las ocho. | *The class begins at eight.* |
| Mañana será viernes. | *Tomorrow will be Friday.* |
| Hoy es el tres de marzo. | *Today is March 3rd.* |
| Es tarde. | *It is late.* |
| Es invierno. | *It is winter.* |

To show ownership, relationship, or what something is made of, the verb **ser** is used.

| | |
|---|---|
| Marta es la hermana de Javier. | *Marta is Javier's sister.* |
| No es mi lápiz; es tuyo. | *It is not my pencil; it's yours.* |
| La pulsera es de plata. | *The bracelet is made of silver.* |

To express the idea of *It's just that . . . .*, or *The fact is that . . . .*, the expression **Es que . . . .** is used by many Spanish speakers.

| | |
|---|---|
| Es que no dormí mucho anoche. | *It's just that I didn't sleep much last night.* |
| Es que no estudian mucho. | *The fact is that they don't study a lot.* |

The verb **ser** is used with impersonal expressions which take the form of **ser + adjective**.

| | |
|---|---|
| Es importante llegar a tiempo. | *It is important to arrive on time.* |
| Es bueno que trabajes tanto. | *It is good that you work so much.* |

## Uses of the Verb Estar

The verb **estar** expresses some state which is more transitory or subject to change. For this reason, it is not used before nouns. Rather than describing the "norm" or the basic essence of a person or thing, it is used to describe conditions that are subject to change or deviations from the norm. The duration of the state described by **estar** is not important. The verb **estar** can be used to describe states that are in existence for minutes, hours, days, or centuries.

Ella está contenta porque celebra su cumpleaños hoy.
*She is happy because she is celebrating her birthday today.*

Diego está nervioso ahora porque va a tener un examen.
*Diego is nervous now because he is going to have an exam.*

Estoy triste porque saqué una mala nota.
*I am sad because I got a bad grade.*

Aquellas montañas siempre están cubiertas de nieve.
*Those mountains are always covered by snow.*

No quiero decirle que están muertos.
*I don't want to tell him that they are dead.*

The verb **estar** is often used to make subjective statements about someone or something. It may be used to reflect one's perception about what is being described. It can also be used to express a change in state or perception. In this way, **estar** is often used to express how something looks, tastes, or feels from the speaker's perspective. Ayllón, Smith, and Morillo (1992:22) provide a very succinct explanation of this distinction by noting that when **ser** is used, "we indicate that we view the subject as a member of a particular class or group, whereas with **estar** we offer a personal comment on the subject without relating it to that class or group."

| | |
|---|---|
| El pollo es delicioso. | *Chicken is delicious.* |
| El pollo está delicioso. | *This chicken (that I am eating) is delicious.* |
| Las manzanas son caras. | *Apples are expensive (generally speaking).* |
| Las manzanas están caras. | *The (these) apples are expensive (comparatively).* |
| Marisol es gorda. | *Marisol is (a) fat (person).* |
| Marisol está gorda. | *Marisol looks fat (or has gained weight).* |
| Eres alto. | *You are (a) tall (person).* |
| ¡Estás alto! | *You've grown!* |
| Marcos es sucio. | *Marcos is (a) dirty (person) (in general).* |
| Marcos está sucio. | *Marcos is dirty.* |

With the exception of describing where an event takes place, and a couple of less common uses which are not significant enough to merit attention here, the verb **estar** is used to denote the location of people, places and things.

Mi casa está en Monroe. *My house is in Monroe.*
Los estudiantes están en el aula. *The students are in the classroom.*

**Exercise 1.** Fill in the blank with the correct form of **ser** or **estar**.

1. ¿Cómo _____ tu papá hoy?
2. No _____ necesario que hablen con él.
3. Yo siempre _____ gordo después de comer en este restaurante.
4. Esta pulsera _____ de Juana.
5. Mi hermana _____ muy amable.
6. El partido _____ en el gimnasio. _____ a las cinco.
7. ¿Cómo _____ la comida en tu país?
8. ¡Esta sopa _____ riquísima!
9. Michael Jordan _____ muy atlético.
10. Me duele el estómago y _____ mareado.
11. ¡Ten cuidado! Esta escalera _____ de madera.
12. Luisiana _____ muy húmedo, pero nos gusta vivir aquí.
13. Su hermano no tiene trabajo porque _____ muy perezoso.
14. El bistec _____ un poco crudo, pero me gusta.
15. Ella _____ contenta con la situación.

## Adjectives that Change Meaning with Ser and Estar

Some adjectives seem to "change meanings" depending upon whether **ser** or **estar** is used. Below are some of these verbs along with their common English translations. Note that in each case **ser** and **estar** retain their basic uses as describing usual characteristics or conditions.

| | |
|---|---|
| Esta clase es muy aburrida. | *This class is very boring.* |
| No estoy aburrido en esta clase. | *I am not bored in this class.* |
| Estamos listos para ir de compras. | *We are ready to go shopping.* |
| No nos engañaron; somos listos. | *They didn't fool us; we are clever.* |

**Meaning-Change Adjectives**

| Adjective | Ser | Estar |
|---|---|---|
| abierto | *frank* | *open* |
| aburrido | *boring* | *bored* |
| atento | *courteous* | *attentive* |
| ciego | *blind* | *blinded (for the moment)* |
| callado | *taciturn (by nature)* | *silent* |
| cansado | *tiresome* | *tired* |
| consciente | *aware* | *conscious (not asleep)* |
| distraído | *absent-minded* | *distracted* |
| interesado | *selfish* | *interested* |
| loco | *insane* | *frantic* |
| libre | *free (without constraints)* | *unoccupied, available* |
| listo | *clever* | *ready* |
| molesto | *annoying* | *bothered* |
| nuevo | *(brand) new* | *new (in appearance)* |
| seguro | *safe* | *certain* |
| triste | *pathetic* | *sad* |
| verde | *green* | *green (not ripe)* |
| vivo | *sharp, lively* | *alive* |

**Exercise 2.** Fill in the blank with the correct form of **ser** or **estar**.

1. ¿Dónde_____ tus hijos?

2. Mi abuela no_____ joven.

3. _____ una escuela excelente.

4. Tus padres_____ muy enojados.

5. ¡Qué bonita_____! ¿Es un vestido nuevo?

6. Este barrio no_____muy seguro.

7. Los vegetales_____buenos para la salud.

8. Hace cinco años que trabajo aquí. Yo_____muy feliz.

9. Nosotros_____de Colombia.

10. El vino de esta región_____muy bueno.

11. ¿Dónde_____la fiesta anoche?

12. Generalmente mi esposa habla mucho, pero hoy_____callada.

13. Mi sobrino_____muy listo y trabajador.

14. Ella_____triste a causa del accidente de su mamá.

15. Ese hombre_____muy abierto; siempre dice la verdad.

**Exercise 3.** Fill in the blank with the correct form of the **ser** or **estar**.

1. El hombre sufrió un trágico accidente, pero todavía_____vivo.

2. ¡Esta comida_____fría!

3. Este cuarto_____sucio. No puedo creerlo; esa chica_____muy limpia.

5. Vamos a salir. ¿_____lista, Juana?

6. Nadie vive en esa casa; _____abandonada.

7. Nos gusta invitarla a nuestras fiestas porque _____ muy viva.

8. Este suéter_____de algodón.

9. La agricultura_____muy importante para Luisiana.

10. Luisiana_____un estado muy bonito.

11. Elena_____la prima de Roberto, ¿verdad?

12. ¿Cómo_____la fiesta anoche?

13. No puedo comer más. _____satisfecho.

14. La fiesta_____aquí en mi casa. ¿Dónde_____tú?

15. No me gusta ese restaurante porque la comida no_____buena.

**Exercise 4.** Translate the following to Spanish.

1. The poor boy didn't know where his mother was.

2. We love to learn. It's just that we didn't bring our books.

3. Yes, I am awake, but this program is boring.

4. He doesn't like the class, but at least he is courteous.

5. The ceremony will be at the church.

6. I know that professors are absent-minded, but that is ridiculous.

7. Under the light in this room, your eyes are very blue.

8. If he left work at nine, Marcos is drunk.

9. It is difficult to tell them that I am worried.

10. The store is open now, but you need to hurry.

# The Passive and Resultant Condition

**The True Passive**

Both Spanish and English have two voices to indicate whether the subject of a sentence is the receiver of the action or the performer of the action. In active voice sentences the subject performs the action expressed by the verb. The major focus in active voice sentences is on the performer of the action (the subject) rather than on the receiver of the action (the direct object). In passive voice sentences the subject is acted upon by someone or something else, and the main focus is shifted to the receiver of the action. In these cases, the direct object in the active voice sentence becomes the subject of the passive voice sentence.

| Active Voice | Passive Voice |
|---|---|
| *John hit the ball.* | *The ball was hit by John.* |
| *Mary ate the cherries.* | *The cherries were eaten by Mary.* |

The "true" passive construction in Spanish is formed by using the verb **ser + past participle**. The passive is used in Spanish when the performer of the action is either expressed or strongly implied. Because the past participle functions as an adjective in passive sentences, it agrees in gender and number with the subject of the sentence.

| | |
|---|---|
| Esta casa fue construída por mi papá. | *This house was built by my father.* |
| Los cuentos fueron escritos por Poe. | *The stories were written by Poe.* |
| Las cartas fueron mandadas por Juan. | *The letters were sent by Juan.* |

It should be noted that the passive voice is much more common in English than in Spanish. In fact, students would be well advised to use the passive very sparingly in Spanish. There are some common alternatives to the passive voice in situations where the performer of the action is not emphasized. These include the use of passive/impersonal **se** construction or the third-person plural verb form.

| | |
|---|---|
| Se venden carros aquí. | *Cars are sold here.* |
| Se habla español en Miami. | *Spanish is spoken in Miami.* |
| Abrirán el restaurante en mayo. | *They will open the restaurant in May.* |
| Necesitan limpiar las calles. | *They need to clean the streets.* |

**Estar with Resultant Condition**

There is another Spanish construction which can be translated in English in the same way as the passive voice. This construction, sometimes referred to as the "apparent" passive or resultant condition, uses the past participle forms with the verb **estar** rather than **ser**. The difference between the two constructions has to do with the fact that the "true" passive emphasizes that an action took place, while **estar** with the past participle emphasizes the result of an action.

La ventana fue rota (por alguien).
*The window was broken (by someone).*

Cuando llegamos a la casa, la ventana estaba rota.
*When we arrived at the house, the window was broken.*

El restaurante fue cerrado (por el dueño).
*The restaurant was closed (by the owner).*

Íbamos a comer en ese restaurante, pero estaba cerrado.
*We were going to eat in that restaurant, but it was closed.*

Keep in mind that the verbs **ser** and **estar** may also be used with the past participle in a tense other than preterit.

La carta será escrita por mi mamá. *The letter will be written by my mother.*
Para el lunes la carta estará escrita. *By Monday the letter will be written.*

**Summary of Uses of Ser and Estar**

| **Uses of Ser** | **Uses of Estar** |
|---|---|
| Origin | Location (except for events) |
| Nationality | Physical or mental condition |
| Profession | Progressive tenses |
| Religion | Resultant condition |
| Relationship | |
| Days/Dates | |
| Material/Purpose | |
| Telling time | |
| Location of events | |
| Usual characteristics | |
| Es que . . . . | |
| Passive voice | |
| Impersonal expressions | |

**Exercise 5.** Translate the following sentences to Spanish.

1. I know that someone is here because the windows are open.

_____

2. Generally he is very happy, but tonight he's angry.

_____

3. The food will be prepared by Marta's aunt.

4. Did you get a haircut? You look handsome.

5. It is good that they don't have time to think about that.

6. The soldiers were already dead when the general arrived.

7. This bottle is empty. It doesn't surprise me that you are drunk.

8. It's just that I was very thirsty.

9. It was summertime when we met.

10. The door was closed, but I didn't know it.

## Lexical Differences

### PEDIR/PREGUNTAR/HACER PREGUNTAS

**Pedir**-*ask for (something), to order (in a restaurant)*

When used with the meaning of *to ask for*, the verb **pedir** takes an object.

| | |
|---|---|
| Yo pedí una taza de café. | *I asked for a cup of coffee.* |
| ¿El café? Yo se lo pedí. | *The coffee? I asked her for it.* |
| | |
| ¿Le pides dinero a tu papá? | *Do you ask your dad for money?* |
| Sí, pero él nunca me lo da. | *Yes, but he never gives it to me.* |

**Preguntar**-*to request information*

| | |
|---|---|
| Ella me preguntó si quería ir al cine. | *She asked me if I wanted to go to the movies.* |
| Yo le voy a preguntar dónde está el baño. | *I am going to ask her where the bathroom is.* |

**Hacer una pregunta**-*to ask a question*

This expression is used to refer to the action of asking a question.

Si no entiendes la lección, haz una pregunta.
*If you don't understand the lesson, ask a question.*

Ella hace muchas preguntas porque es inteligente.
*She asks a lot of questions because she is intelligent.*

**Exercise 6.** Translate the following sentences to Spanish.

1. She asked me where I lived.

2. They were very quiet this morning.

3. Although she is always nervous at parties, she talks to everyone.

4. I'm not going to buy these tomatoes; they're green.

5. When I ask her a question she gets mad.

6. If you want the job, you have to ask him for it.

7. My old friend Marcos always asks me for money.

8. If you ask me that one more time, I am going to scream.

9. He is so tall! I can't believe he has grown so much.

10. I'm free this afternoon if you want to come with me to the mall.

# CHAPTER 6

# Adjectives

## Adjectives and Adjective Formation

An adjective is used to modify a noun or pronoun by limiting or qualifying its meaning. Adjectives can be divided into two categories: descriptive and limiting adjectives. Generally speaking, adjectives in Spanish have four forms which agree in gender and number with the noun that is being modified. Adjectives whose masculine singular form ends with **-o** have a corresponding feminine form that ends in **-a**. The plural of these adjectives is formed by adding **-s** to the singular forms.

| Adjectives With Masculine Singular –o Ending | | |
|---|---|---|
| | Singular | Plural |
| **Masculine** | el libro **rojo** | los libros **rojos** |
| **Feminine** | la casa **roja** | las casa **rojas** |

Many adjectives have only one singular form. These are made plural by adding **-s** if the singular form ends in a vowel, and **-es** if it ends in a consonant. Adjectives that end in **-ista** are invariable for gender; they add **-s** for the plural. If two nouns of different genders are modified by the same adjective, the masculine plural form is used.

| | |
|---|---|
| La clase es interesante. | *The class is interesting.* |
| El libro es interesante. | *The book is interesting.* |
| | |
| Los hombres son corteses. | *The men are courteous.* |
| Las mujeres son corteses. | *The women are courteous.* |
| | |
| El examen es fácil. | *The exam is easy.* |
| Los exámenes son fáciles. | *The exams are easy.* |
| | |
| Ella es muy optimista. | *She is very optimistic.* |
| Él es muy optimista. | *He is very optimistic.* |

An **-a** is added to form the feminine of adjectives of nationality or adjectives that end in **-án, dor,** and **ón.**

| | |
|---|---|
| Las mujeres francesas leen mucho. | *French women read a lot.* |
| Los hombres franceses hablan mucho. | *French men talk a lot.* |
| | |
| El chico es muy preguntón. | *The boy is very inquisitive.* |
| La chica es muy preguntona. | *The girl is very inquisitive.* |

A few adjectives have only one form. These include **modelo** 'model', **sport** 'sports', **hembra** 'female', **macho** 'male', **beige** 'beige', and **alerta** 'alert'. Modified color nouns such as **verde oscuro** 'dark green', **azul marino** 'light blue', and **azul marino** 'navy blue' are also invariable.

| | |
|---|---|
| No voy a comprar los pantalones beige. | *I am not going to buy the beige pants.* |
| Nuestros enemigos están alerta. | *Our enemies are alert.* |
| Pueden usarse camisas azul marino. | *Navy blue shirts may be worn.* |
| Nos gustan los coches sport. | *We like sports cars.* |

## Apocopation

Apocopation is the shortening of a word by dropping a letter or letters from the end of the word. The adjectives **uno, bueno, malo, alguno, ninguno, primero,** and **tercero** drop the final **-o** before masculine singular nouns. However, when they precede forms other than masculine singular, or when they follow the noun, they use their complete forms.

| | |
|---|---|
| un libro | *one/a book* |
| unos libros | *some books* |
| un buen chico | *a good boy* |
| los chicos buenos | *the good boys* |

Apocopation occurs with the adjectives **grande, ciento,** and **cualquiera** when they precede a noun of either gender. The adjective **grande** means *great* when it precedes the noun and **large** when it follows.

| | |
|---|---|
| la gran mujer | *the great woman* |
| las ciudades grandes | *the large cities* |
| los grandes soldados | *the great soldiers* |
| el gran músico | *the great musician* |
| cien pesetas | *one hundred pesetas* |

The adjective **Santo** 'saint' becomes **San** before masculine proper names with the exception of those that begin with **To-** or **Do-**.

| | | | |
|---|---|---|---|
| San Juan | Santo Domingo | Santo Tomás | San Marcos |

**Exercise 1.** Fill in the blank with the correct form of the adjective.

| | |
|---|---|
| 1. los hombres_____ | (honest) |
| 2. una_____escritora | (great) |
| 3. los chicos_____ | (pessimistic) |
| 4. unas jirafas_____ | (female) |
| 5. una chica_____ | (talkative) |
| 6. los bomberos_____ | (alert) |
| 7. los zapatos_____ | (black) |
| 8. _____Marta | (Saint) |
| 9. _____libro interesante | (a) |
| 10. _____sillas | (one hundred) |
| 11. las chicas_____ | (English) |
| 12. mis amigos_____ | (Spanish) |
| 13. la mesa y el pupitre_____ | (new) |
| 14. las clases_____ | (special) |
| 15. los hombres_____ | (French) |
| 16. el_____chico | (good) |
| 17. _____Pedro. | (Saint) |
| 18. el_____día | (third) |
| 19. un_____profesor | (great) |
| 20. las camisas_____ | (light blue) |

## Position of Descriptive Adjectives

Descriptive adjectives are used to indicate something about the basic nature of the nouns they modify. They describe characteristics such as shape, size, shape, color, nationality, and religion. As you learned early in your study of Spanish, descriptive adjectives generally follow the nouns they modify. However, descriptive adjectives may also precede the nouns in many cases. Whether an adjective precedes or follows the noun may be determined by meaning, stylistic effect, dialect differences, or simply conventional usage.

William Bull (1965: 20) makes the observation that an unmodified noun has "a referential potential that is theoretically infinite." In other words, it represents all the possible referents of that noun. When one uses a descriptive adjective to modify a noun, it may describe all of the referents of the noun at the same time, or it may describe only some of its referents. In other words, one can describe the entire set of referents or a subset of the total. This distinction is signaled not by any change in the adjective itself, but by its syntactic position.

When the definite article marks totality and describes all the referents of the noun, the adjective precedes the noun. In this case, the major emphasis is on the noun itself. It may be said that the adjective is being used to describe rather than to specify. Prenominal position is favored when the speaker wishes to convey that the adjective reflects a characteristic that is somehow expected or is inherent to the meaning of the noun itself. It is often the case that the adjective will be placed before the noun if the adjective is being used in a figurative sense.

In postnominal position, however, it is the adjective which receives more emphasis. As postnominal position may be considered the "stronger" position for the adjective relative to the noun, when the adjective follows the noun, it is used in a more literal sense and has a more objective connotation.

In considering whether or not an adjective should precede or follow a noun, it may be helpful to distinguish whether the adjective is being used restrictively or nonrestrictively. Nonrestrictive adjectives are those that refer to the totality of the noun being modified. They are used to indicate an inherent quality of the noun rather than to distinguish it from others of its kind. The definite article combines with adjectives in prenominal position to indicate totality.

**Nonrestrictive**

el famoso autor de *El Aleph*  (There is only one author of this book.)
*the famous author of El Aleph*

la blanca nieve  (There is no contrast with snow of other colors)
*the white snow*

las magníficas ruinas de Uxmal  (These are the only ones.)
*the magnificent ruins of Uxmal*

el terrible accidente  (There is no contrast with less severe accidents.)
*the terrible accident*

mi querida esposa  (I have only one.)
*my beloved wife*

la suave brisa  (There is no contrast with stronger breezes.)
*the gentle breeze*

los distinguidos profesores  (There is no contrast with less distinguished ones.)
*the distinguished professors*

el frío invierno  (There is no contrast with warmer ones.)
*the cold winter*

The most common position for descriptive adjectives is after the noun. Placing the adjective after the noun implies a partitive connotation, meaning that only some of the referents share the characteristic. In postnominal position the adjective functions to specify or restrict the entities under consideration.

**Restrictive**

| | |
|---|---|
| un vestido rojo<br>*a red dress* | (as a subset of all possible dresses) |
| una chica simpática<br>*a nice girl* | (as compared to others) |
| los empleados trabajadores<br>*the hardworking employees* | (as opposed to the ones who are lazy) |
| las casas grandes de este barrio<br>*the large houses of this neighborhood* | (as compared to the smaller ones) |
| mi hija inteligente<br>*my intelligent daughter* | (as compared to my other less-gifted daughter) |
| tu carro bonito<br>*your pretty car* | (as compared to your other one that is ugly) |
| un problema difícil<br>*a difficult problem* | (as compared to others we have faced) |

When considering adjective placement, one must take into account the entities under consideration. If one is speaking figuratively about all the beautiful waterways of Louisiana, it would be possible to say the first sentence below. On the other hand, if one is comparing the size of several of Louisiana's rivers, thereby limiting or restricting the possible entities under consideration, one would need to place the adjective after the noun. Remember also that a speaker chooses his or her own reality which may be different in the opinion of others, as illustrated by the last two sentences below.

Prefiero pescar en los bonitos ríos de Luisiana.
*I prefer to fish in the beautiful rivers of Louisiana.*

Prefiero pescar en los ríos pequeños de Luisiana.
*I prefer to fish in the small rivers of Louisiana (not the larger ones).*

Ella quiere recordar a los hombres guapos de Luisiana.
*She wants to remember the handsome men of Louisiana (not the ugly ones).*

Ella quiere recordar a los guapos hombres de Luisiana.
*She wants to remember (all) the handsome men of Louisiana (not contrastive).*

## Adjectives that Change Meaning According to Placement

For English speakers some adjectives appear to change meanings depending upon their position relative to the nouns they modify. In many cases, the prenominal adjective has a more figurative, subjective, or emotional connotation, whereas postnominal placement suggests a more literal or objective meaning. Listed below are some adjectives that change meaning depending upon whether they are placed before or after the nouns they modify.

| Adjective | Meaning If Follows Noun | Meaning If Precedes Noun |
|---|---|---|
| antiguo | ancient, antique | former |
| grande | large | great |
| medio | average | half |
| nuevo | brand new | different |
| pobre | poor | unfortunate |
| triste | sad | pitiful, meager |
| único | unique | only |
| viejo | old (age) | old, longstanding |

**Exercise 2.** Place the correct form of the adjective before or after the noun according to the meaning of the sentence.

1. Ella me compró una _____ camisa _____ .  (red)
2. El _____ pintor _____ de este cuadro vivía en Francia.  (famous)
3. Los _____ estudiantes _____ son listos.  (French)
4. Ella quiere comer _____ pescado _____ .  (fried)
5. Juan y yo somos _____ amigos _____ .  (old)
6. Los _____ amores _____ duran para siempre.  (great)
7. En _____ años _____ los precios han subido.  (recent)
8. Mi esposa es una _____ mujer _____ .  (sensitive)
9. Los _____ hombres _____ necesitan ejercicio también.  (old)
10. Me encanta visitar las _____ ruinas _____ de Tulum.  (ancient)
11. Mi _____ esposo _____ trabaja demasiado.  (beloved)
12. Sé emborrachó después de beber _____ botella _____ de vino.  (half)
13. Ellos sufrieron una _____ tragedia _____ .  (terrible)

14. Mi _____ papá _____ siempre me ayudaba.  (good)
15. El _____ problema _____ que tenemos es la pereza.  (only)
16. La _____ tía _____ de Juan va a darle dinero.  (favorite)
17. Le dijeron de la _____ muerte _____ de su papá.  (tragic)
18. Me gustan los _____ estudiantes _____ de ULM.  (nice)
19. El _____ millonario _____ nunca será feliz.  (poor)
20. El _____ clima _____ de Luisiana es bueno para la agricultura.  (pleasant)
21. La _____ religión _____ predomina en los pueblos.  (Catholic)
22. Necesito un _____ carro _____ .  (cheap)
23. Nos gusta visitar las _____ montañas _____ de Colorado.  (tall)
24. Las _____ sábanas _____ están en mi cuarto.  (clean)
25. Le ofrecemos nuestra _____ disculpa _____ .  (sincere)

**Exercise 3.** Translate the following to Spanish.

1. We don't like to buy old cars.
_____

2. I'll always remember the white cliffs of Dover.
_____

3. This summer I plan to read a lot of interesting books.
_____

4. The unforgettable Dr. Jones always gave hard tests.
_____

5. Our beautiful daughter is studying in France.
_____

6. My former boss used to say that I needed to work more.
_____

7. Her true passion was helping children.
_____

8. Great men and women learn from their mistakes.
_____

9. I like big cars, but I don't like to pay for the gasoline.

___

10. Famous artists never complain about the lack of money.

___

## Limiting Adjectives

Limiting adjectives most often describe quantity, location, or possession. They include the demonstrative adjectives, possessive adjectives, numbers, and other adjectives of quantity. In general, limiting adjectives precede the nouns they modify. Examples of these include **mucho**, **poco**, **varios**, and **bastante**, as well as the ordinal and cardinal numbers.

| | |
|---|---|
| Hay muchos estudiantes en la clase. | *There are many students in the class.* |
| Tengo dos hermanos. | *I have two brothers.* |
| Esta clase es muy interestante. | *This class is very interesting.* |
| Mis padres trabajan en una fábrica. | *My parents work in a factory.* |
| El primer día de clase fue muy difícil. | *The first day of class was difficult.* |
| No tengo bastante información. | *I don't have enough information.* |

## Possessive Adjectives

Possessive adjectives, as their name implies, are used with the noun to talk about possession or to whom the noun belongs. The possessive adjective agrees with the noun that is possessed, not with the possessor. In Spanish there are two forms of the possessive adjective: the short forms and the long forms. The short forms are used much more frequently.

| Short-Form Possessive Adjectives | |
|---|---|
| **Singular** | **Plural** |
| mi(s) | nuestro(a)(os)(as) |
| tu(s) | vuestro(a)(os)(as) |
| su(s) | su(s) |

All short-form possessive adjectives agree in number with the nouns they modify, but only the first and second-person plural forms agree in gender. In the case of the third-person singular and plural adjectives, there is a possibility of ambiguity if the meaning is not clarified by the context of the discussion. This ambiguity can be resolved by using the preposition **de** and a prepositional pronoun.

No tengo mi libro.
*I don't have my book.*

Quieren venir a nuestra casa.
*They want to come to our house.*

Son sus amigos.
Son los amigos de él (ella, usted, ellos, ellas, ustedes).
*They are his/her/your (formal)/their (masc.)/their (fem.) /your (plural)/friends.*

Voy a hablar con su mamá.
Voy a hablar con la mamá de ella, (ellos, etc.)
*I am going to talk with her (their, etc.) mother.*

| **Long-Form Possessive Adjectives** | |
|---|---|
| mío, mía, míos, mías | nuestro, nuestra, nuestros, nuestras |
| tuyo, tuya, tuyos, tuyas | vuestro, vuestra, vuestros, vuestras |
| suyo, suya, suyos, suyas | suyo, suya, suyos, suyas |

The long-form possessive adjectives follow the nouns they modify and agree in gender and number with the noun. They are generally used for stylistic effect by emphasizing the possessor of the noun under consideration. For this reason, they are sometimes called "stressed" or "strong" possessives.

Las opiniones tuyas son extrañas. *Your opinions are strange.*
Un amigo mío viene de Baton Rouge. *A friend of mine is coming from Baton Rouge.*
No tengo los libros tuyos. *I don't have your books.*

**Possessive Pronouns**

The possessive pronouns are formed by combining the definite article and the long-form possessive adjectives. Both the definite article and the possessive adjective agree with the noun that is being replaced. The definite article is generally omitted after the verb **ser**.

No necesitas mis llaves. *You don't need my keys.*
Las tuyas están en la mesa. *Yours are on the table.*

¿De quién es la mochila? *Whose is the backpack?*
No sé. La mía está aquí. *I don't know. Mine is here.*
No es mi camisa. Es suya. *It is not my shirt. It is his.*

## Lexical Differences

**FELIZ/ALEGRE/CONTENTO**

**Feliz**-*happy, contented*

The adjective **feliz** is used to talk about happiness in the sense of something that is more profound or longer-lasting. For this reason, it is used most often with the verb **ser**.

**Contento**-*happy (about something)*

When one wishes to express the idea that someone is happy about something at a particular time, the adjective **contento** is used. Because it describes a more transitory state, it is generally used with the verb **estar**.

**Alegre**-*happy*

There appears to be more variation with regard to the use of **alegre** than with **contento** and **feliz**. However, as its usage seems to more closely resemble that of **contento** in most cases, it used more often with the verb **estar**.

Nos casamos hace cinco años. Somos muy felices.
*We got married five years ago. We are very happy.*

Ella está contenta porque acaba de recibir una beca.
*She is happy because she just received a scholarship.*

Estoy alegre porque me aumentaron el sueldo.
*I am happy because they gave me a raise.*

**Exercise 4.** Translate the following to Spanish.

1. I don't have anything, but I am happy.

2. We don't know where your gloves are. Ours are here in the car.

3. Whose bottle of beer is this? Don't look at me. It's not mine.

4. She is not happy because her boyfriend told her that he was going to leave her.

5. Uxmal was a ceremonial center for the Mayas.

_____

6. Juan just bought a brand new car.

_____

7. *Don Quijote*, the excellent novel written by Cervantes, is very famous.

_____

8. If you listen to the wise advice of your parents, you won't have problems.

_____

9. The honest lawyer refused to accept the money we offered him.

_____

10. Our efficient secretary always knows where the important documents are.

_____

# CHAPTER 7

# The Subjunctive in Noun Clauses

## Formation of the Subjunctive Tenses

### Regular Present Subjunctive Forms

The present subjunctive is conjugated using the first-person singular stem of the present tense and adding **-e, -es, -e, -emos -éis**, and **-en** for regular **-ar** verbs. The endings for **-er** and **-ir** verbs are **-a, -as, -a, -amos, áis**, and **-an**.

| Regular Present Subjunctive Conjugations | | |
|---|---|---|
| **Hablar** | **Comer** | **Vivir** |
| hable | coma | viva |
| hables | comas | vivas |
| hable | coma | viva |
| hablemos | comamos | vivamos |
| habléis | comáis | viváis |
| hablen | coman | vivan |

### Spelling-Change Verbs in the Present Subjunctive

The present subjunctive for verbs that end in **-car, -gar**, or **-zar** will have the same spelling-change irregularity as in the preterit (**c to qu, g to gu**, and **z to c**). In the present subjunctive, however, the change occurs in every form.

| Present Subjunctive Conjugations: Spelling-Change Verbs | | |
|---|---|---|
| **Buscar** | **Llegar** | **Empezar** |
| busque | llegue | empiece |
| busques | llegues | empieces |
| busque | llegue | empiece |
| busquemos | lleguemos | empecemos |
| busquéis | lleguéis | empecéis |
| busquen | lleguen | empiecen |

**Irregular Subjunctive Forms**

**Stem-Changing Present Subjunctive Forms**

The **-ar** and **-er** stem-changing verbs will have a change in every form of the present subjunctive except for the **nosotros** and **vosotros**.

**Present Subjunctive Conjugations: -AR and -ER Stem-Changing Verbs**

| Pensar | Volver |
|---|---|
| piense | vuelva |
| pienses | vuelvas |
| piense | vuelva |
| pensemos | volvamos |
| penséis | volváis |
| piensen | vuelvan |

The **-ir** verbs that have a stem change in the present indicative will have a stem change in the present subjunctive. This stem change will follow the regular pattern as described above, except that the **nosotros** and **vosotros** forms will have a change of either **e to i** or **o to u**.

**Present Subjunctive Conjugations: -ER and -IR Stem-Changing Verbs**

| Pedir | Dormir |
|---|---|
| pida | duerma |
| pidas | duermas |
| pida | duerma |
| pidamos | durmamos |
| pidáis | durmáis |
| pidan | duerman |

## Other Irregular Present Subjunctive Forms

Some verbs in the present subjuntive are completely irregular.

**Present Subjunctive Conjugations: Irregular Verbs**

| Dar | Estar | Ir |
|---|---|---|
| dé | esté | vaya |
| des | estés | vayas |
| dé | esté | vaya |
| demos | estemos | vayamos |
| deis | estéis | vayáis |
| den | estén | vayan |

| Ser | Saber | Haber |
|---|---|---|
| sea | sepa | haya |
| seas | sepas | hayas |
| sea | sepa | haya |
| seamos | sepamos | hayamos |
| seáis | sepáis | hayáis |
| sean | sepan | hayan |

**Exercise 1.** Give the correct present subjunctive forms.

1. yo (to be able to) _____
2. tú (to bring) _____
3. él (to be (sick)) _____
4. ellos (to do, make) _____
5. ustedes (to read) _____
6. Juan y yo (to think) _____
7. tú (to work) _____
8. yo (to sleep) _____
9. yo (to know people) _____
10. usted (to give) _____
11. tú (to go) _____
12. su mamá (to come) _____
13. mi tío (to know facts) _____
14. Marcos (to order) _____
15. mis amigos (to have) _____
16. tus padres (to be (tall)) _____
17. yo (to drink) _____
18. nosotros (to sleep) _____
19. ella (to eat) _____
20. usted (to drive) _____

**Imperfect Subjunctive**

The past subjunctive forms are based on the third-person plural of the preterit indicative. To form the imperfect subjunctive, the **-ron** of the of the preterit ending is removed and the following endings added: **-ra, -ras, -ra, -ramos, -rais,** and **-ran.** The **nosotros** forms will carry a written accent.

| Imperfect Subjunctive Conjugations: Regular Verbs | | |
|---|---|---|
| **Hablar** | **Comer** | **Vivir** |
| hablara | comiera | viviera |
| hablaras | comieras | vivieras |
| hablara | comiera | viviera |
| habláramos | comiéramos | viviéramos |
| hablarais | comierais | vivierais |
| hablaran | comieran | vivieran |

**Exercise 2.** Give the imperfect subjunctive form of the following verbs in the person indicated.

1. ella (to have) _____

2. nosotros (to sleep) _____

3. tú (to know) _____

4. mi papá (to go) _____

5. tus primos (to come) _____

6. yo (can, to be able to) _____

7. ellos (to work) _____

8. ella (to see) _____

9. usted (to eat) _____

10. nuestra mamá (to cook) _____

11. su amigo (to buy) _____

12. el profesor (to read) _____

13. yo (to ask for, order) _____

14. ustedes (to bring) _____

15. nosotros (to serve) _____

16. usted (to build) _____

17. tú (to say, tell) _____

18. ella (to hear) _____

19. ella (to convince) _____

20. yo (to catch) _____

## Present Perfect and Past Perfect Subjunctive

The present perfect subjunctive is formed with present subjunctive of **haber + past participle**. The past perfect subjunctive is formed with the past subjunctive of **haber + past participle**.

**Present Perfect Subjunctive**

| Hablar | Comer | Vivir |
|---|---|---|
| haya hablado | haya comido | haya vivido |
| hayas hablado | hayas comido | hayas vivido |
| haya hablado | haya comido | haya vivido |
| hayamos hablado | hayamos comido | hayamos vivido |
| hayáis hablado | hayáis comido | hayáis vivido |
| hayan hablado | hayan comido | hayan vivido |

**Past Perfect Subjunctive**

| Hablar | Comer | Vivir |
|---|---|---|
| hubiera hablado | hubiera comido | hubiera vivido |
| hubieras hablado | hubieras comido | hubieras vivido |
| hubiera hablado | hubiera comido | hubiera vivido |
| hubiéramos hablado | hubiéramos comido | hubiéramos vivido |
| hubierais hablado | hubierais comido | hubierais vivido |
| hubieran hablado | hubieran comido | hubieran vivido |

**Exercise 3.** Give the present perfect or imperfect perfect subjunctive form of the following verbs.

1. mi novia (had eaten) _____
2. ustedes (had left) _____
3. él (has broken) _____
4. yo (have seen) _____
5. usted (had said) _____
6. ellos (had died) _____
7. tú (have made) _____
8. usted y yo (have opened) _____
9. ella (has written) _____
10. tus primos (had read) _____

## Subjunctive Mood and Indicative Mood

Mood is an indication of a speaker's attitude toward some action or condition through the use of distinct verbal forms. There are three verbal moods in Spanish: indicative, subjunctive, and imperative. Both English and Spanish have these three moods, but few English speakers are familiar with exactly what the subjunctive mood is or how it is used. For the most part, this can be attributed to two facts about the subjunctive in English. First of all, the subjunctive is not used very much at all in English. Whitley (1986: 118) suggests that its usages are "relics" and that the subjunctive is "moribund" in English. Secondly, the following examples show that in the few cases where Standard English still requires a subjunctive the forms are not uniquely identifiable as subjunctive.

Ojalá que fuera rico.
*I wish I were rich.*

Ella insiste en que se quede hasta las nueve.
*She insists that he stay until nine.*

The subjunctive is used frequently in Spanish. Spanish speakers must distinguish experiences that are known, experienced, or inferred from those that are unknown, not experienced, or not inferred. Use of the indicative mood asserts the independent existence of a statement; the subjunctive reveals that a statement is dependent on another expression. If the speaker views what he or she is saying as factual, relatively certain, or objective, the indicative mood is used. If it is uncertain, possible, subjective, or hypothetical, the subjunctive is used. Generally speaking there are four basic uses of the subjunctive in Spanish: to indicate that one person is attempting to influence the actions of another; to express an emotional reaction to facts; to express doubt, disbelief, denial, or uncertainty; and to express a subjective viewpoint about a particular statement.

The subjunctive often reveals that a speaker has doubts concerning the validity of an assertion or about the possibility of something happening or being done. It gives known facts the color of subjectivity and deals with the realm of personal feeling, mental reservation, or uncertainty. Because of the dependence between the speaker's feeling about the action and the action itself, the subjunctive is used primarily in dependent or subordinate clauses introduced by the conjunction **que**. Dependent clauses have a conjugated verb, but they cannot stand alone as a sentence; they can function as nouns, adjectives, or adverbs.

Sé que ellos estudian mucho.                    (known)
*I know that they study a lot.*

Dudo que ellos estudien mucho.                  (unknown)
*I doubt that they study a lot.*

Tengo una novia que baila bien.                 (experienced)
*I have a girlfriend who dances well.*

Busco una novia que baile bien.                 (not-experienced)
*I am looking for a girlfriend who dances well.*

# The Subjunctive in Noun Clauses

A noun clause is one that takes the place of the noun in another phrase or clause. Because noun clauses function as nouns, they can take the position of nouns in a sentence, serving as the subject or object of the verb. The subjunctive is used in noun clauses when the verb in the main clause expresses doubt, disbelief, emotion, uncertainty, desire, or when suggestions are made to influence the actions of another person.

| | |
|---|---|
| Quiero esa casa. | *I want that house.* |
| Quiero que compres esa casa. | *I want you to buy that house.* |
| | |
| Conozco a ese hombre. | *I know that man.* |
| Conozco al hombre que vive en esa casa. | *I know the man who lives in that house.* |

## The Subjunctive with Imposition of Will

When the verb in the main clause indicates that the subject is attempting to influence the actions of someone else, the subjunctive will be used in the subordinate clause. Verbs of volition include verbs of wanting, suggesting, recommending, asking, begging, pleading, requesting, and desiring. With these constructions, the subjunctive will be used in both negative and affirmative sentences. It is important to remember that English often uses the infinitive in these cases. Students must learn not to translate word for word sentences that involve imposition of will.

| | |
|---|---|
| Yo prefiero que ella se quede aquí. | *I prefer that she stay here.* |
| Mi profesor me aconseja que estudie. | *My professor advises me to study.* |
| No queremos que salgas. | *We don't want you to leave.* |
| Juan quiere que yo vaya. | *Juan wants me to go.* |
| Ana le pidió que se quedara. | *Ana asked him to stay.* |

If there is no change of subject in sentences expressing imposition of will, the infinitive is used in Spanish.

| | |
|---|---|
| Ella prefiere que traigas la comida. | *She prefers that you bring the food.* |
| Ella prefiere traer la comida. | *She prefers to bring the food.* |
| | |
| Yo no quiero que limpies el baño. | *I don't want you to clean the bathroom.* |
| Yo no quiero limpiar el baño. | *I don't want to clean the bathroom.* |

With the verbs **dejar, exigir, impedir, mandar, permitir,** and **prohibir** the infinitive may be used even if there is a change of subject.

| | |
|---|---|
| Ellos no permiten que salgamos. | *They don't allow us to go out.* |
| Ellos no nos permiten salir. | |
| | |
| Ella les exige que se queden. | *She demands that they stay.* |
| Ella les exige quedarse. | |

| **Verbs of Volition** | | | |
|---|---|---|---|
| aconsejar | *to advise* | pedir | *to ask for, request* |
| dejar | *to allow* | permitir | *to permit* |
| desear | *to want* | preferir | *to prefer* |
| esperar | *to hope* | prohibir | *to prohibit* |
| exigir | *to require, demand* | querer | *to want* |
| impedir | *to prevent* | recomendar | *to recommend* |
| insistir en | *to insist* | rogar | *to beg* |
| mandar | *to order* | sugerir | *to suggest* |
| necesitar | *to need* | | |

**The Subjunctive with Emotional Reaction**

The subjunctive is used in dependent clauses after expressions that convey an emotional response or subjective viewpoint. With these expressions, the subjunctive is used in both affirmative and negative sentences. The following are some of the verbs which denote expressions of emotion.

| **Verbs of Emotional Reaction** | | | |
|---|---|---|---|
| alegrarse de | *to be glad* | molestar | *to bother* |
| gustar | *to please* | sentir | *to be sorry* |
| lamentar | *to regret* | sorprender | *to surprise* |

| | |
|---|---|
| Siente que estés enfermo. | *He is sorry that you are sick.* |
| Me alegro de que vayan. | *I am glad that they are going.* |
| No nos gusta que lleguen tarde. | *We don't like that they arrive late.* |

As was the case with imposition of will, the infinitive is used with expressions of emotional reaction if the subject in the main clause is the same as the subject in the subordinate clause. In these cases it does not matter whether the sentence is affirmative or negative.

| | |
|---|---|
| Siento llegar tarde. | *I am sorry to have arrived late.* |
| No le gusta hacer muchas preguntas. | *He does not like to ask a lot of questions.* |
| Me alegro de estar aquí. | *I am glad to be here.* |

**The Subjunctive with Doubt, Disbelief, and Denial**

The subjunctive is used in noun clauses when the verb expresses doubt, disbelief, denial, or a negation of reality. With doubt, disbelief, and denial, changing the verb in the main clause to affirmative or negative will change the mood of the subordinate clause.

| Expressions of Doubt, Disbelief, and Denial | | | |
|---|---|---|---|
| no creer | *not to believe* | no es claro | *it is not clear* |
| dudar | *to doubt* | no es evidente | *it is not evident* |
| negar | *to deny* | no es seguro | *it is not certain* |
| no pensar | *not to think* | no es verdad | *it is not true* |
| no es cierto | *it is not certain* | no puede ser | *it can't be* |

Dudamos que vayan.     *We doubt that they are going.*
No dudamos que van.     *We don't doubt they are going.*

Mi papá no cree que trabajemos.     *My dad doesn't think that we work.*
Mi papá cree que trabajamos.     *My dad thinks that we work.*

No es verdad que sean flojos.     *It is not true that they are lazy.*
Es verdad que son flojos.     *It is true that they are lazy.*

Niega que estén en casa.     *He denies that they are home.*
No niega que están en casa.     *He does not deny that they are home.*

**The Subjunctive with Impersonal Expressions**

In Spanish, the subjunctive is used with certain expressions which indicate emotional reaction, subjectivity, or what is or is not possible. These expressions, sometimes called *impersonal expressions*, take the form **ser + adjective + que**. If these expressions occur in the main clause, the subordinate clause will be in the subjunctive mood unless the expression denotes truth or certainty. Examples of expressions which denote certainty include **es verdad que**, **es cierto que**, **es seguro que**, and **es evidente que**. The following are examples of impersonal expressions which require the subjunctive in the subordinate clause. Keep in mind that the verb **ser** need not be in the present tense.

Es malo que no te hayan llamado.     *It is bad that they have not called you.*
Era importante que comiera más.     *It was important for her to eat more.*
Será necesario que lleguen temprano.     *It will be necessary for them to arrive early.*

| Impersonal Expressions | | | |
|---|---|---|---|
| es agradable que | *it is nice* | es malo que | *it is bad* |
| es bueno que | *it is good* | es natural que | *it is natural* |
| es curioso que | *it is odd* | es necesario que | *it is necessary* |
| es estupendo que | *it is great* | es normal que | *it is normal* |
| es increíble que | *it is incredible* | es posible que | *it is possible* |
| es importante que | *it is important* | es preciso que | *it is necessary* |
| es imposible que | *it is impossible* | es preferible que | *it is preferable* |
| es interesante que | *it is interesting* | es probable que | *it is probable* |

## The Subjunctive with "Ojalá que"

**Ojalá (que)** is a common expression meaning *I hope* or *I wish*. It is always followed by the subjunctive. If what is hoped for is possible, or not contrary-to-fact, **Ojalá que** is used with the present or present perfect subjunctive and is translated as *I hope*. If the desired situation is contrary-to-fact, the imperfect or past perfect subjunctive is used, and **Ojalá** is translated as *I wish*.

Ojalá que estudie más.                (possible, not contrary-to-fact)
*I hope she studies more.*

Ojalá que haya estudiado más.         (possible, not contrary-to-fact)
*I hope she has studied more.*

Ojalá que estudiara más.              (not the case, contrary-to-fact)
*I wish she would study more.*

Ojalá que hubiera estudiado más.      (not the case, contrary-to-fact)
*I wish she had studied more.*

**Exercise 4.** Give the correct present subjunctive, present indicative, or infinitive form.

1. Necesito que Juan_____(to clean) el baño.
2. No voy a_____(to leave) una propina.
3. Ellos no dudan que nosotros_____(study).
4. Nos sorprende que ella no_____(know) la lección.
5. Lamento_____(to be) aquí.
6. Me gusta que ella_____(has worked) tanto.
7. Preferimos_____(to eat supper) más tarde.
8. No es necesario que él_____(speak) tanto.
9. Ella espera_____(to travel) a España con nosotros.
10. Sabemos que ella_____(does) su tarea.
11. Ella niega que nosotros_____(have) que trabajar.
12. No es verdad que ellos_____(complain) todos los días.
13. Te pido que me_____(give) el cuaderno.
14. Ella prefiere que nosotros_____(to choose) el color.
15. Es curioso que tú _____(buy) carros viejos.

## Sequence of Tenses

When it is determined that the subjunctive is needed in a particular sentence, one must then decide which subjunctive tense is required. It stands to reason that the correspondence of tenses between the main clause and the subordinate clause must be a logical one. When deciding which subjunctive tense to use, the sequence of tenses is a very useful guide. In general, present tense indicative verbs in the main clause will be accompanied by present tense subjunctive verbs in the subordinate clause; past indicative tenses in the main clause will have past subjunctive forms in the subordinate clause. In order to understand the sequence of tenses, one must first become familiar with which tenses are present tenses and which are past tenses.

**Present and Past Tenses**

| Present Tense Set | Past Tense Set |
|---|---|
| Present | Preterit |
| Present Perfect | Imperfect |
| Future | Conditional |
| Future Perfect | Past Perfect |
|  | Conditional Perfect |

The sequence of tenses requires that if the subjunctive is needed in a particular sentence and the verb in the main clause is in one of the tenses included in the present tense set, then the verb in the subordinate clause will be in the present subjunctive or the present perfect subjunctive. If the verb in the main clause is in one of the tenses of the past set, then the verb in the subordinate clause will be either imperfect subjunctive or pluperfect subjunctive. If the main verb is in the imperative and the subjunctive is required, the verb in the subordinate clause will be either present or present perfect subjunctive.

| | |
|---|---|
| Quiero que Juan vaya. | *I want Juan to go.* |
| Ella nos pedirá que llamemos. | *She will ask us to call.* |
| Les hemos dicho que se queden. | *We have told them to stay.* |
| Le dijimos a Juan que fuera. | *We told Juan to go.* |
| Dudaba que ella viniera. | *He doubted that she would come.* |
| No habría ido si hubiera llovido. | *I would not have gone if it had rained.* |
| No te levantes hasta que hayan salido. | *Don't get up until they have left.* |

In some unusual cases, following the sequence of tenses would create sentences in which there would not be a logical correspondence between the verbs in the main and subordinate clauses. In noun clauses this sometimes occurs with verbs of knowing, believing, or doubting. In these cases, the subjunctive tense is determined not by the tense of the verb in the main clause, but by the time the event actually occurred relative to the verb in the main clause.

| | |
|---|---|
| Dudo que Juan estuviera en casa anoche. | *I doubt Juan was at home last night.* |
| No creo que fuera al cine ayer. | *I don't think he went to the movies yesterday.* |

| Sequence of Tenses | |
|---|---|
| **Main Clause Indicative Tense** | **Subordinate Clause Subjunctive** |
| Present | |
| Present Perfect | Present |
| Future | Present Perfect |
| Future Perfect | |
| Commands | |
| | |
| Preterit | |
| Imperfect | |
| Past Perfect | Imperfect |
| Conditional | Past Perfect |
| Conditional Perfect | |

**Exercise 5.** Fill in the blank with the correct tense of the subjunctive or indicative mood or the infinitive. Do not rely exclusively on the English translation in parentheses.

1. Pablo espera que tú_____ ( will translate) las cartas.
2. Es verdad que ellos no_____ (work) mucho.
3. Era posible que ellos_____ (had arrived).
4. No creíamos que usted_____ (would go) a la fiesta.
5. Insistí en que ellos_____ (bring) el postre.
6. No dudábamos que ellos_____ (had) las herramientas.
7. Siempre había querido_____ (to visit) España.
8. Era increíble que tú _____ (would want) ir.
9. Nos gustaba que ellos_____ (had made) la ensalada.
10. Tengo miedo que ustedes_____ (are going) a decírselo.
11. Pidió que yo_____ (buy) el suéter.
12. Cree que nosotros_____ (have) miedo.
13. Siento que ustedes no lo_____ (have seen).
14. No negó que yo_____ (could) ganarlo.
15. Es evidente que ellos_____ (are leaving) mañana.
16. Sabíamos que ellos_____ (had sold) el coche.
17. Insistían en que yo_____ (take) la foto.

18. Yo voy a dejar que ellos_____ (give) la fiesta.
19. No dudaba que ella siempre_____ (studied) mucho.
20. Le pedí a Julio que_____ (to sing).
21. Me alegré de que ellos_____ (had gone) contigo.
22. No es seguro que él_____ (will come) mañana.
23. Juan desea_____ (to go) al cine esta noche.
24. Pensaba que ellos_____ (would tell) la verdad.
25. Me gustaría que ustedes_____ (to stay) aquí.

**Exercise 6.** Translate the following sentences to Spanish.

1. At this moment you don't need to study but to pray.
_____

2. Yes, I heard a noise outside, but I was afraid to look.
_____

3. Besides, I want to wait until you get home.
_____

4. Before going to the party, he decided to tell his wife about the little accident.
_____

5. We don't work to buy what we want but what we need.
_____

6. After asking him for money, they decided to buy him a gift.
_____

7. She doubts that I am in love with her.
_____

8. I know that I said that, but life has changed a lot since that day.
_____

9. By Monday they will have put my furniture outside.
_____

10. She looks very much like her lovely mother.
_____

**Exercise 7.** Translate the following sentences to Spanish.

1. We don't think he knows how to drive.

2. I was glad that you did not go.

3. He had asked her to wait here for a few minutes.

4. I didn't want the doctor to give him a shot.

5. I'm sorry that you can't come until tomorrow night.

6. They wanted you to write the letter for them.

7. It is true that she has a lot of money, but she is stingy.

8. She prefers that we stay here tonight.

9. Do you (formal) want me to sign the check?

10. I hope they go to that restaurant because the food is delicious.

**Exercise 8.** Translate the following sentences to Spanish.

1. They wanted us to leave early, but we had to work.

2. I advise you (familiar) to try on the dress before buying it.

3. We recommend that you (familiar) go to class early.

_____

4. She doesn't doubt that he is a good boy.

_____

5. They were glad that he had put on his shoes.

_____

6. ¿Do you (plural) hope to return by nine?

_____

7. It is sad that they have already left.

_____

8. We would like them tell the truth.

_____

9. We were hoping that she would send us the tickets.

_____

10. It can't be that they have stolen the money.

_____

## Lexical Differences

### PERO/SINO

**Pero**-*but (nevertheless)*

This conjunction is most often used to join two independent clauses. It restricts the meaning of the first statement, but it does not contradict it.

| | |
|---|---|
| Quiero ir, pero me quedo en casa. | *I want to go, but I'm staying home.* |
| Estudia mucho, pero saca malas notas. | *He studies a lot, but he gets bad grades.* |
| Ella es inteligente pero floja. | *She is intelligent but lazy.* |

**Sino**-*but (instead)*

**Sino** is used when the first part of a sentence is negative and contradicts the second part.

Ella no habla francés sino español.
*She does not speak French but (instead) Spanish.*

No voy al banco sino al correo.
*I am not going to the movies, but (instead) to the post office.*

When two contradictory clauses are joined, the conjunction **sino que** must be used.

Ella no estudió anoche, sino que fue a la fiesta con su novio.
*She did not study last night, but (instead) she went to the party with her boyfriend.*

No regresé a la casa temprano, sino que trabajé dos horas más.
*I didn't return to the house early, but (instead) I worked two hours more.*

One must be careful with sentences in which the first negative clause is not contradicted by the second. These will require **pero** rather than **sino**.

No ganaron el partido, pero jugaron bien. *They didn't win the game, but they played well.*
No trabajé mucho, pero estoy cansado. *I didn't work a lot, but I'm tired.*

**Exercise 9.** Translate the following sentences to Spanish.

1. She doesn't live far away, but I don't like to walk.

2. Why don't you do something instead of complaining so much?

3. He said that they had talked to her before leaving the house.

4. She didn't go out last night but she stayed here at home.

5. They didn't bring wine but beer.

6. I told you that we had burned the papers.

7. We were going to call you, but we remembered that you had to study.

8. She wanted to wait until he had taken a shower.

9. After talking with our attorney, we decided to move to Dallas.

10. They have gone to the store for bread because you ate it all up.

# CHAPTER 8

# The Subjunctive in Adjective and Adverbial Clauses

## The Subjunctive with Adjective Clauses

An adjective clause is a subordinate clause that functions as an adjective and is introduced by a relative pronoun.

Queremos comprar un coche **grande**.                    (adjective)
*We want to buy a large car.*

Queremos comprar un coche **que tenga cuatro puertas**.    (adjective clause)
*We want to buy a car that has four doors.*

With adjective clauses the **que** functions as a relative pronoun rather than a conjunction as is the case with noun clauses. The antecedent of the adjective clause determines whether the verb in the subordinate clause is indicative or subjunctive. If the antecedent refers to a specific or definite entity whose existence is asserted, the verb in the main clause will be in the indicative. If the antecedent does not exist, or if its existence is uncertain, the subjunctive is used.

Yo tengo un amigo que me da dinero.
*I have a friend who gives me money.*

Yo necesito un amigo que me dé dinero.
*I need a friend who will give me money.*

Buscan una secretaria que hable ruso.
*They are looking for a secretary who speaks Russian.*

Buscan a la secretaria que habla ruso.
*They are looking for the secretary who speaks Russian.*

Conocemos a alguien que tiene conocimiento de computadoras.
*We know someone who has knowledge of computers.*

No conocemos a nadie que tenga conocimiento de computadoras.
*We don't know anyone who has knowledge of computers.*

**Exercise 1.** Fill in the blank with the correct tense and mood.

1. Ella buscaba al hombre que_____ese coche.   (drives)
2. Nosotros tenemos un libro que nos_____ mucho.   (cost)
3. Necesito un profesor que me _____con la tarea.   (will help)
4. No había nadie que_____la tarea.   (had finished)
5. Prefiero ir a un restaurante que_____comida china.   (serves)
6. Necesito llamar a mi amigo que_____en Inglaterra.   (lives)
7. No quería salir con una chica que_____.   (smoked)
8. Hay muchas personas aquí que_____rápido.   (drive)
9. ¿Tienes amigos que_____cocinar?   (know how to)
10. Pensaba encontrar un lugar que_____ más tranquilo.   (would be)

## The Subjunctive with Adverbial Clauses

Adverbial clauses are subordinate clauses that are introduced by an adverbial conjunction. As is the case with adverbs, adverbial clauses modify the verb in the main clause with regard to time, manner, place, purpose, or condition.

| | |
|---|---|
| Estudiamos por la tarde. | *We study in the afternoon.* |
| Estudiamos cuando tenemos tiempo. | *We study when we have time.* |
| | |
| Trabajo para ganar dinero. | *I work to earn money.* |
| Trabajo para que puedas comer. | *I work so that you can eat.* |

In Spanish the adverbial conjunctions can be divided into two categories: those that are always followed by the subjunctive, and those that are sometimes followed by the subjunctive. The "sometimes" conjunctions will be followed by the subjunctive if the verb in the main clause is in the future or future perfect tense or if it implies future action. The present tense, the periphrastic future (**ir a + infinitive**), and the imperative can be used to imply future action.

### Adverbial Conjunctions that Sometimes Take the Subjunctive

| | |
|---|---|
| cuando | *when* |
| tan pronto como | *as soon as* |
| después que | *after* |
| hasta que | *until* |

| Adverbial Conjunctions that Always Take the Subjunctive | |
|---|---|
| para que | *in order that* |
| a fin de que | *so that* |
| a menos que | *unless* |
| salvo que | *except* |
| antes de que | *before* |
| sin que | *without* |
| con tal de que | *provided that* |
| en caso de que | *in case that* |

Yo voy a salir tan pronto como lleguen mis padres.
*I am going to leave as soon as my parents arrive.*

Ellos no comieron hasta que llegaron sus amigos.
*They did not eat until their friends arrived.*

Ella vendrá a la fiesta cuando terminemos el trabajo.
*She will come to the party when we finish the work.*

¿Te dormiste después que te llamé?
*You fell asleep after I called you?*

Llámame cuando los veas.
*Call me when you see them.*

    If the subject is the same for both the main clause and the subordinate clause, the corresponding prepositional form and an infinitive are used instead of the subjunctive. Listed below are the conjunctions with the corresponding prepositional forms.

| Conjunction Versus Preposition | |
|---|---|
| **Conjunction** | **Preposition** |
| antes (de) que | antes de |
| después que | después de |
| para que | para |
| sin que | sin |

| | |
|---|---|
| No voy a salir sin que me vean. | *I am not leaving without their seeing me.* |
| No voy a salir sin verlos. | *I am not leaving without seeing them.* |
| | |
| Llamaremos después que lleguen. | *We will call after they arrive.* |
| Llamaremos después de llegar. | *We will call after arriving (we arrive).* |

**Exercise 2.** Fill in the blank with the correct infinitive, subjunctive or indicative form.

1. Yo esperé para que ellos_____verme.  (could)
2. Diles que se_____aquí.  (to stay)
3. Ellos van a salir sin_____.  (eating)
4. Cuando nosotros_____, vamos a contártelo todo.  (return)
5. Ella se acostó después que_____su novio.  (left)
6. Generalmente me quejo hasta que él_____.  (arrives)
7. Dudaba que ella_____del accidente.  (knew)
8. Ella lo hacía antes de que sus hijos_____.  (got up)
9. Juana compró el aceite para_____las papas.  (cook)
10. Yo no bebo agua cuando_____sed.  (have)

## The Subjunctive with "If Clauses"

"If clauses" are adverbial clauses that modify the verb of the main clause. The indicative is used in the "if clause" when the information is presented as not being contrary-to-fact. The subjunctive is used in "if clauses" to present a situation that is contrary-to-fact. However, the easiest way to deal with "if clauses" is to remember that the subjunctive will be used in an "if clause" only when the verb in the main clause is in the conditional or the conditional perfect tense.

Only the imperfect subjunctive or the past perfect subjunctive may be used in "if clauses;" neither the present subjunctive nor the present perfect subjunctive can be used. As the following chart illustrates, it is relatively simple to know when to use the subjunctive or indicative in "if clauses."

### Rule for "If Clauses"

| If the verb in the main clause is: | The verb in the "if clause" will be: |
|---|---|
| Present | Present Indicative |
| Conditional | Imperfect Subjunctive |
| Conditional Perfect | Past Perfect Subjunctive |

## The Subjunctive with "As If" Clauses

The expression *as if* is translated in Spanish as **como si**. "**Como si**" clauses introduce situations that are contrary-to-fact. For this reason, they will always be followed by the imperfect or past perfect subjunctive.

El hombre nos hablaba como si supiera todo.
*The man talked to us as if he knew everything.*

Nos recibió como si nos hubiera conocido antes.
*He received us as if he had met us before.*

**Exercise 3.** Fill in the blank with the correct tense and mood forms. Remember that you cannot rely exclusively on the English translation in parentheses.

1. Era necesario que él_____menos. (eat)
2. Espero que ustedes_____a tiempo. (will arrive)
3. Sentía que ellos lo_____. (had mistreated)
4. Yo siempre_____la televisión cuando ella estudia. (watch)
5. Ella dudaba que yo_____a la fiesta. (would come)
6. Yo iría al cine si_____más dinero. (had)
7. Saldremos tan pronto como ella nos_____. (calls)
8. Yo lo hice para que ellos_____la lección. (would learn)
9. Les sorprende que ella_____treinta años. (have)
10. Era imposible que nosotros_____a Europa. (would go)
11. No dudo que ella_____hacerlo. (can)
12. Busco un estudiante que_____mucho. (studies)
13. Era bueno que ella_____. (had registered)
14. Juan le pidió a Ana que_____. (sit down)
15. Yo_____, pero necesito estudiar. (would go)
16. No conozco a nadie que_____ocho idiomas. (speaks)
17. Pienso que tú_____cocinar. (know how)
18. Ella quería que nosotros le_____dinero. (give)

19. Sabían que ella_____muy simpática.     (was)
20. Es posible que Juan_____el piano.     (will play)
21. Yo comeré antes de que ellos_____.     (have finished)
22. Ella llamó después que él_____.     (had left)
23. Me gusta el fútbol, pero siempre_____cuando era niño.     (lost)
24. Me alegraba que ella_____la comida en la mesa.     (had put)
25. Era malo que ellos no_____su tarea.     (had done)

**Exercise 4.** Translate the following sentences to Spanish.

1. We did not know that you had studied in France.

2. It surprises me that you have cleaned your room.

3. I gave you the money so that you could buy food.

4. They asked him to leave.

5. They didn't think that you had returned.

6. We will be here until they call us.

7. It was impossible for us to go with them.

8. We were looking for an employee who would work more.

9. It was evident that they did not know the truth.

10. She wanted to greet him without our seeing her.

## Lexical Differences

### SACAR/QUITAR/QUITARSE/LLEVAR/TOMAR

**Sacar**-*to take something out* or *to remove something (from inside something else)*

| | |
|---|---|
| Yo saqué dinero de mi bolsa. | *I took money out of my purse.* |
| Saca la basura esta tarde. | *Take out the trash this afternoon.* |

**Quitar**-*to take something away (from someone)*

| | |
|---|---|
| El hombre le quitó el dulce al niño. | *The man took the candy from the boy.* |
| Me quitaron el dinero. | *They took the money from me.* |

**Quitarse**-*to take off clothes*

| | |
|---|---|
| Me quité la camisa. | *I took off my shirt.* |
| Se quitaron los zapatos. | *They took off their shoes.* |

**Llevar**-*to take (someone or something to a place); to wear*

| | |
|---|---|
| Voy a llevarte conmigo. | *I am going to take you with me.* |
| Necesitas llevar vino a la fiesta. | *You need to take wine to the party.* |
| Ella llevaba un vestido azul. | *She was wearing a blue dress.* |

**Tomar**-*to take (ingest) something* or *to take a mode of transportation*

| | |
|---|---|
| Toma la medicina, hijo. | *Take the medicine, son.* |
| Voy a tomar un taxi hoy. | *I am going to take a taxi today.* |

**Exercise 5.** Translate the following to Spanish.

1. I doubt that they are taking her with them to the party tomorrow night.

2. The father took the money from his children.

3. We had asked them to give her a bath.

4. They knew the man who had robbed the bank.

5. She would have taken the medicine earlier, but she had to go to the pharmacy.

6. It was great that she had already sent them the package.

7. If they don't know how to drive, they need to stay home.

8. I wish they would leave her alone.

9. They were looking for a mechanic who spoke Spanish.

10. She didn't doubt that he could cook.

11. If they had asked me, I would have told them.

12. She was acting as if she were the owner of the restaurant.

13. We were sorry that they had lost the game.

14. She would have taken the children to the park, but it was raining.

15. She hopes to spend Christmas with her family.

# CHAPTER 9

# Other Uses of the Subjunctive and Commands

## The Subjunctive in Concessive Sentences

There are a few expressions that may require the subjunctive or the indicative depending on the intended meaning. The expressions **aunque** and **a pesar de que** take the indicative if they refer to something that is considered to be a fact. In this case they are often translated as *even though, although* or *in spite of (the fact that)*. The subjunctive is used with these expressions if they are being used to denote conjecture or supposition. They are usually translated by the English expression *even if* in these cases.

Aunque estoy cansado, sigo trabajando.  (I am tired.)
*Even though I am tired, I continue working.*

Aunque esté cansado, iré al centro.  (It is possible that I'll be tired.)
*Even if I am tired, I will go downtown.*

Comeremos a pesar de que no nos gusta la comida.  (We don't like the food.)
*We will eat even though we don't like the food.*

Comeremos a pesar de que no nos guste la comida.  (It is possible that we won't like it.)
*We will eat even if we don't like the food.*

## The Subjunctive in Independent Clauses

The subjunctive is sometimes used in independent clauses with expressions of wishing, leave-taking, or as indirect commands.

| | |
|---|---|
| ¡Que te diviertas! | *Have a good time!* |
| Que le vaya bien. | *I hope it goes well for you.* |
| Que Dios los acompañe. | *May God be with you.* |
| Que hable Juan. | *Let Juan speak.* |
| Que lo coma Mikey. | *Let Mikey eat it.* |

The subjunctive is also sometimes used after the expressions *tal vez* and *quizá(s)*. Whether or not the subjunctive is used will depend upon the degree of doubt the speaker wishes to convey.

Juan no fue a la fiesta. Tal vez está enfermo.
*Juan didn't go to the party. He may be (is probably) sick.*

Juan no fue a la fiesta. Quizás esté enfermo.
*Juan didn't go to the party. He may (possibly) be sick.*

## The Imperative Mood

**Formal Commands**

The affirmative **usted** commands are formed by using the third-person singular of the present subjunctive. The **ustedes** commands are are formed by taking the third-person plural of the present subjunctive.

| Usted/Ustedes Commands | | |
|---|---|---|
| **Affirmative** | **Negative** | |
| **Singular** | hable | No hable |
| **Plural** | hablen | No hablen |
| **Singular** | coma | No coma |
| **Plural** | coman | No coman |
| **Singular** | escriba | No escriba |
| **Plural** | escriban | No escriban |

Because their forms are based on the present subjunctive, the following **usted/ustedes** command forms are also irregular.

| Irregular Usted/Ustedes Commands | | |
|---|---|---|
| | usted | ustedes |
| dar | dé | den |
| ir | vaya | vayan |
| estar | esté | estén |
| ser | sea | sean |
| saber | sepa | sepan |

**Exercise 1.** Give the correct **usted** or **ustedes** command forms.

1. usted (Don't go) _____
2. usted (Look) _____
3. ustedes (Don't buy) _____
4. ustedes (Know) _____
5. usted (Write) _____
6. usted (Tell) _____
7. ustedes (Arrive) _____
8. ustedes (Take out) _____
9. ustedes (Follow) _____
10. usted (Don't lose) _____
11. ustedes (Don't put) _____
12. usted (Make) _____
13. usted (Be (smart)) _____
14. ustedes (Read) _____
15. usted (Don't give) _____
16. usted (Leave) _____
17. usted (Bring) _____
18. usted (Don't forget) _____
19. ustedes (Speak) _____
14. ustedes (Wear) _____

**Informal Commands**

The regular affirmative **tú** commands are the same as the third-person singular of the present indicative tense. The negative **tú** commands are the same as the second-person singular of the present subjunctive. The following **tú** commands are irregular in the affirmative, but their negative forms follow the regular rule.

| Irregular Tú Command Forms | | |
|---|---|---|
| | **Affirmative** | **Negative** |
| poner | pon | No pongas |
| tener | ten | No tengas |
| venir | ven | No vengas |
| ir | ve | No vayas |
| decir | di | No digas |
| ser | sé | No seas |
| salir | sal | No salgas |
| hacer | haz | No hagas |

| | |
|---|---|
| No les digas eso. | *Don't tell them that.* |
| Escríbeme pronto. | *Write to me soon.* |
| ¡Llega a tiempo! | *Arrive on time!* |
| Haz la tarea. | *Do the homework.* |
| Pon la comida en la mesa. | *Put the food on the table.* |

**Exercise 2.** Give the correct **tú** command form.

1. Send_____
2. Have_____
3. Put_____
4. Turn off_____
5. Don't come_____
6. Do_____
7. Don't cry_____
8. Don't play_____
9. Don't tell_____
10. Ask for, order_____
11. Leave_____
12. Don't be (nervous) _____
13. Don't read _____
14. Go_____
15. Follow_____
16. Wait_____
17. Don't look_____
18. Bring_____
19. Don't make_____
20. Don't pick up_____

The affirmative **vosotros** commands for **-ar**, **-er**, and **-ir** verbs are formed by removing the infinitive ending and adding **–ad**, **-ed**, and **–id**, respectively. The negative **vosotros** command is the second-person plural form of the present subjunctive.

| Vosotros Command Forms | |
| --- | --- |
| Affirmative | Negative |
| hablad | no habléis |
| comed | no comáis |
| escribid | no escribáis |

## First-Person Plural (Nosotros) Commands

Both the affirmative and negative **nosotros** commands are formed by using the first-person plural of the present subjunctive. The verbs **ir** and **irse** become **vamos** and **vámonos** in the affirmative imperative. However, in the negative they follow the regular rule.

| Nosotros Command Forms | | |
|---|---|---|
| | Affirmative | Negative |
| hablar | hablemos | no hablemos |
| comer | comamos | no comamos |
| escribir | escribamos | no escribamos |

## Position of Pronouns with Commands

Direct object, indirect object, and reflexive pronouns precede negative commands and are attached to the affirmative commands.

| | | |
|---|---|---|
| Háblanos | *Speak to us.* | (informal) |
| No lo comas. | *Don't eat it.* | (informal) |
| Escríbales. | *Write to them.* | (formal) |
| No se levante. | *Don't get up.* | (formal) |
| Hagámoslo. | *Let's do it.* | (nosotros) |

When an affirmative **nosotros** command is used with the pronouns **nos** and **se**, the final **-s** of the command form is dropped. In the negative **nosotros** command, these forms do not change.

| | |
|---|---|
| Acostémonos. | *Let's go to bed.* |
| No nos acostemos. | *Let's not go to bed.* |
| | |
| Callémonos. | *Let's be quiet.* |
| No nos callemos. | *Let's not be quiet.* |
| | |
| Mandémoselo. | *Let's send it to him.* |
| No se lo mandemos. | *Let's not send it to him.* |

**Exercise 4.** Translate the following commands to Spanish.

1. ¿El dinero? _____, André.      (Send it to us)

2. ¿Los boletos? _____, señor.      (Return them to her)

3. _____ al cine esta noche.      (Let's go)

4. ¿El programa? _____, niños.           (Don't watch it)
5. _____ aquí.                            (Let's sit)
6. _____ ahora, mi amor.                  (Let's get up)
7. ¿La pulsera? _____, Juan.              (Don't buy it for her)
8. _____ todo el dinero, Marisol.         (Don't lose)
9. _____, niños.                          (Take a bath)
10. ¿Ese cuento? _____.                   (Let's read it to them)
11. _____ a clase temprano, estudiantes.  (Arrive)
12. _____ la tarea para las seis, Ana.    (Do)
13. ¿La cuenta? _____, señor.             (Bring it to me)
14. ¿Las ropas? _____, Juan.              (Pick them up)
15. No _____ aquí, señor.                 (Don't sit)

**Exercise 5.** Translate the following sentences to Spanish.

1. I need the salt. Pass it to me, Mom.

_____

2. If you like that car, buy it for her, Carlos.

_____

3. We want to hear the story. Tell us what happened, guys.

_____

4. Let's not wait until they have left.

_____

5. They always ask you for money. Don't send it to them, Dad.

_____

6. Go to bed before 9:00, kids.

_____

7. The shoes are pretty. Try them on, madam.

_____

8. Tell them to take care of the children, Marisol.

_____

9. We don't have the documents, Mr. Rodriguez. Bring them to us.

_____

10. Don't worry so much, Ana.

_____

11. Let's hurry up before they realize that we don't have tickets.

_____

12. That shirt is ugly. Don't show it to her, Antonio.

_____

## Lexical Differences

### PONERSE/VOLVERSE/HACERSE/LLEGAR A SER

In Spanish there are several verbs which are used to express the idea *to become*. Very subtle changes in the meaning may be conveyed depending on which verb is used. According to Christopher Pountain (2003: 125), the most versatile of these are **volverse** and **hacerse**, with **hacerse** being restricted to "processes which can be thought of as in some way natural or expected."

**Hacerse**-*to become*

Use of **hacerse** generally implies voluntary will or effort. It is commonly used for religious, professional, or political changes.

| | |
|---|---|
| Se hizo católica. | *She became (a) Catholic.* |
| Mi hijo se hizo arquitecto. | *My son became an architect.* |

**Ponerse**-*to become*

This verb is used to indicate a change of mood, physical condition or appearance. With the exception of the expression **ponerse viejo**, the changes expressed by **ponerse** are usually short-lived. It is used to mark the beginning point of states with which one would use the verb **estar**. **Ponerse**, like the verb **estar**, emphasizes the transitory nature of a change. As is also the case with **estar**, one cannot use the verb **ponerse** with nouns.

| | |
|---|---|
| Ella se puso contenta. | *She became happy.* |
| Ellos se pusieron enojados. | *They became angry.* |
| Mi mamá se puso pálida. | *My mom turned pale.* |

As the box below indicates, there are quite a number of pronominal verbs which may be used to express to idea of *to become*. In most cases, these verbs are used in the same way as the verb **ponerse**.

| **Pronominal Expressions for *To Become*** | | | |
|---|---|---|---|
| aburrirse | *to get bored* | entristecerse | *to become sad* |
| alegrarse | *to become happy* | entusiasmarse | *to become excited* |
| cansarse | *to get tired* | envejerse | *to get old* |
| callarse | *to get quiet* | fastidiarse | *to become annoyed* |
| emborracharse | *to get drunk* | inquietarse | *to become anxious* |
| enfermarse | *to get sick* | irritarse | *to become irritable* |
| enojarse | *to get angry* | mejorarse | *to get better* |

**Volverse**-*to become*

Use of this verb implies involuntary mental or psychological change when applied to human beings. It is used in circumstances where a change is felt to be more permanent than is the case with **ponerse**. **Volverse**, like the verb **ser**, suggests a more essential or lasting change. The meaning of **volverse** can often be translated by the English *ended up being* or *turned into*. While the verb **volverse** can be used with nouns, its most common usage is with adjectives that can be complements of either **ser** or **estar**. Pountain (2003: 125) suggests that **volverse** is more neutral with adjectives, while **hacerse** is the more neutral form when used with nouns.

The difference between **ponerse** and **volverse** can be compared with the use of the verbs **ser** and **estar**.

Se puso loca cuando le dijeron el precio.
*She went crazy when they told her the price.*

Se volvió loca después de la muerte de su esposo.
*She became insane after the death of her husband.*

**Llegar a ser**-*to become*

Like **hacerse** the expression **llegar a ser** is used when there is a change brought about through one's own efforts. The difference is that **llegar a ser** gives more emphasis to the process, passage of time, or movement from one status level to the next. For this reason, **llegar a ser** is not used for changes that happen suddenly or unexpectedly.

| | |
|---|---|
| El soldado llegó a ser general. | *The soldier became a general.* |
| Juan llegó a ser jefe de su departamento. | *Juan became the boss of his department.* |

**Summary of Verbs Meaning** *To Become*

| Verb | Used With | To Describe |
|---|---|---|
| Hacerse | Nouns or adjectives | Change involving voluntary will or effort; natural or expected changes |
| Volverse | Adjectives (less common with nouns) | An involuntary, longer-lasting mental or psychological change |
| Ponerse | Adjectives | A short-lived change of mood or physical condition |
| Llegar a ser | Nouns or adjectives | Change involving will or effort with emphasis on process or passage of time |

**Exercise 6.** Fill in the blank with the correct form of the appropriate verb for *to become*. In each case, the verb will be in a past tense. In some cases, more than one answer may be possible.

1. Cuando oyó del accidente, ella_____triste.
2. Después de muchos años, él_____presidente de la asociación.
3. Cuando perdió a su hijo, la pobre mujer_____loca.
4. Ese garaje_____escuela.
5. Ellos_____muy sospechosos después del robo.
6. Mi hermano_____músico.
7. Yo_____nervioso cuando llegó el jefe.
8. Ella_____roja al ver su nota en el examen.
9. La mujer_____una bailarina famosa después de treinta años.
10. Yo sabía que ella iba a tener éxito. Ella_____abogada.

**Exercise 7.** Translate the following sentences to Spanish.

1. The ugly duckling became a beautiful swan.

2. She became very quiet when we mentioned the job.

3. I got better, but only after spending two weeks in the hospital.

4. I became happy when they told me about the birth.

5. After learning a lot about their profession, many actors become directors.

6. He got really mad when they criticized the poor politician.

7. Calm down! You get crazy when you talk about this.

8. Josh studied a lot and became and accountant.

9. Ana became depressed and decided to go to the hospital.

10. I get really tired when I don't go to bed early.

# CHAPTER 10

# Adverbs, Prepositions, and Conjunctions

## Adverbs

Adverbs are words that are used to modify or limit verbs, adjectives, other adverbs, or a whole sentence. They are used to indicate time, place, reason, degree, or manner. Many adverbs of manner are formed by adding the suffix **-mente** to the feminine form of the adjective. If an adjective does not show gender, the suffix is added to the singular form. However, some very common adverbs such as **bien**, **mal**, **muy**, **despacio**, and **mucho** are not formed according to this rule.

| Adjective and Adverb Forms | |
|---|---|
| **Adjective** | **Adverb** |
| lento | lentamente |
| rápido | rápidamente |
| evidente | evidentemente |
| especial | especialmente |

| | |
|---|---|
| Hablamos ayer. | *We talked yesterday.* |
| Juega mal. | *He plays badly.* |
| Están aquí. | *They are here.* |
| Generalmente me acuesto tarde. | *I generally go to bed late.* |

In cases where more than one adverb is used to modify the same verb, the **-mente** suffix is added to only the last adverb.

| | |
|---|---|
| Yo manejaba cuidadosamente. | *I was driving carefully.* |
| Ella habló lento y claramente. | *She spoke slowly and clearly.* |

When used with an intransitive or stative verb, an adjective can function in a way that resembles an adverb of manner. In such cases the adjective modifies both the verb and the subject, and it agrees with the subject in gender and number.

| | |
|---|---|
| La chica llegó cansada. | *The girl arrived tired.* |
| Los chicos salieron contentos. | *The boys left happy.* |
| Mi hijo dormía tranquilo. | *My son was sleeping peacefully.* |

In some cases, the masculine singular form of the adjective form can be used in such a way that it modifies only the verb.

| | |
|---|---|
| Ella habló lento. | *She spoke slowly.* |
| Ustedes cantaron bonito. | *You sang prettily.* |

## Prepositions

Prepositions are invariable forms which link one element of a sentence, such as a noun or pronoun, with another element such as a noun, a pronoun, a noun phrase, or an infinitive. Spanish has both simple and compound prepositions.

**Simple Prepositions**

| | | | |
|---|---|---|---|
| a | *to, at* | entre | *between* |
| ante | *before* | hacia | *towards* |
| bajo | *under* | hasta | *until* |
| con | *with* | para | *for, in order to, by, towards* |
| contra | *against* | por | *for, by through, because of* |
| de | *of, from, about* | según | *according to* |
| desde | *since, from* | sin | *without* |
| durante | *during* | sobre | *on, upon, about* |
| en | *at, in, into, on* | tras | *after* |

**Compound Prepositions**

| | | | |
|---|---|---|---|
| a causa de | *because of* | después de | *after (time)* |
| acerca de | *concerning* | detrás de | *behind* |
| a favor de | *in favor of* | encima de | *on top of, above, over* |
| al lado de | *beside* | enfrente de | *in front of* |
| alrededor de | *around (place)* | en vez de | *instead of* |
| antes de | *before* | en cuanto a | *as for* |
| a pesar de | *in spite of* | frente a | *opposite, across from* |
| cerca de | *near* | fuera de | *outside of* |
| debajo de | *below, under(neath)* | junto a | *next to* |
| debido a | *due to* | lejos de | *far from* |
| dentro de | *inside of* | | |

The prepositions themselves often do not have much semantic content; their meanings are largely dependent on context. In some cases, there is a close correspondence between English and Spanish with regard to prepositional usage.

| | |
|---|---|
| Vengo de mi casa. | *I am coming from my house.* |
| Juega con sus amigos. | *He is playing with his friends.* |
| Ella está en la sala. | *She is in the living room.* |

However, in other cases the correspondence between Spanish and English prepositions does not hold. As illustrated by the following examples, the English translation of a preposition in one case may not be the same as its translation in another.

| | |
|---|---|
| Lo vimos en la playa. | *We saw him at the beach.* |
| Ella se casó con Juan. | *She got married to Juan.* |
| Pienso en el examen. | *I am thinking about the exam.* |
| Sueñan con viajar a México. | *They dream about traveling to Mexico.* |

Some transitive verbs in Spanish do not require a preposition where one would be required for the English equivalent.

| | |
|---|---|
| Espero el autobús. | *I am waiting for the bus.* |
| Buscan su tarea. | *They are looking for their homework.* |
| Les pedmios dinero. | *We asked them for money.* |
| Mira la pizarra. | *She is looking at the chalkboard.* |
| El carro lo atropelló. | *The car ran over him.* |

**Exercise 1.** Fill in the blank with the correct preposition.

1. Ellos van a comer_____limpiar la casa.      (before)
2. Compramos una escoba_____barrer el piso.      (in order to)
3. No vamos a terminar la tarea_____el lunes.      (until)
4. La tienda está_____el banco.      (across from)
5. Estamos_____cancelar clase mañana.      (in favor of)
6. Prefiero aprender_____la historia de México.      (about)
7. _____mi situación económica, no puedo ir.      (Due to)
8. Mi esposa puso la propina_____la mesa.      (on top of)
9. _____la presentación fuimos al estadio.      (After)
10. No pudimos pescar_____el viento.      (because of)

**Exercise 2.** Translate the following sentences to Spanish.

1. During the battle, everyone thought about the homeland.

_____

2. According to his mother, Juan is in love with me.

_____

3. Between you and me, they need to talk about the divorce.

___

4. I know that I put the bags under the table.

___

5. They left without knowing what had happened.

___

6. The girls in the class always get mad at me.

___

7. As for me, I want to live far from the city.

___

8. That's fine. I'll put the phone next to my bed.

___

9. We want to sleep instead of watching that boring game.

___

10. She got up and began to walk towards us.

___

**Uses of A**

The preposition **a** is used in Spanish to show movement or direction toward a destination in time or space. This can even include "figurative" movement toward engaging in some activity or influencing someone else to do so.

| | |
|---|---|
| Viajan a México. | *They are traveling to Mexico.* |
| Vuelvo a mi casa. | *I am returning to my house.* |
| La invité a salir. | *I invited her to go out.* |
| Se puso a estudiar. | *She began to study.* |
| Le enseñé a bailar. | *I taught him to dance.* |
| Nos obligaron a limpiar. | *They forced us to clean.* |

The preposition **a** is distinguished from **en** by the fact that **en** is generally used to show location when no motion is involved. Therefore, the English locative *at* is most often translated as **en** in Spanish. However, there are some common expressions in English where the preposition *at* would be translated as **a** in Spanish. These often involve expressions of time, measuring distance, or very close proximity to something.

| | |
|---|---|
| Me senté a la mesa. | *I sat down at the table.* |
| La clase comienza a las nueve. | *The class begins at nine.* |
| Mi casa está a veinte millas de la capital. | *My house is twenty miles from the capital.* |

When used before direct objects that refer to a specific person or persons, this preposition is known as the **personal a**. Note that the **personal a** is not used before non-specific or non-personalized direct objects. In the case of animals there is much variation, depending mainly on how "human-like" the animal is considered to be. The **personal a** is not used with the verb **tener** when it means *to possess*, but it may be used if the meaning of **tener** is *to hold* or *to have someone in a certain place*.

| | |
|---|---|
| Conozco a esa chica. | *I know that girl.* |
| No veo a mis hijos. | *I don't see my children.* |
| Ella buscaba un novio rico. | *She was looking for a rich boyfriend.* |
| Tengo tres hijos. | *I have three children.* |
| Tenemos a mi mamá en nuestra casa. | *We have my mom at our house.* |

The preposition **a** is used to describe the manner in which something is done. However, other prepositions may be used in a similar fashion.

| | |
|---|---|
| Ella vino a mi casa a pie. | *She came to my house on foot.* |
| Las camisas están hechas a mano. | *The shirts are made by hand.* |
| Poco a poco lo haremos. | *Little by little we will do it.* |
| El chico lo hizo a propósito. | *The boy did it on purpose.* |
| Lo mataron a sangre fría. | *They killed him in cold blood.* |

The preposition **a** is used to introduce the indirect object of a sentence.

| | |
|---|---|
| Le di el dinero a mi hijo. | *I gave the money to my son.* |
| Les voy a mandar la carta a mis padres. | *I am going to send the letter to my parents.* |
| | |
| Al ver a su mamá, la chica se puso a llorar. | *Upon seeing her mother, the girl began to cry.* |
| Al llegar al cine, compramos las entradas. | *Upon arriving at the theater, we bought the tickets.* |

| Expressions with the Preposition A | | | |
|---|---|---|---|
| aprender a | *to learn (to do something)* | decidirse a | *to decide to* |
| asistir a | *to attend* | enseñar a | *to teach (someone to do something)* |
| atreverse a | *to dare to* | jugar a | *to play (a game)* |
| ayudar a | *to help (do something)* | oler a | *to smell like* |
| comenzar a | *to begin (to do something)* | parecerse a | *to look like, resemble* |
| dar a | *to face, look out on* | saber a | *to taste like* |

### Uses of De

The preposition **de** is used to describe a point of origin or departure from a place.

| | |
|---|---|
| Ella viene de su casa. | *She is coming from her house.* |
| Yo soy de Perú | *I am from Peru.* |
| Ella salió del cuarto. | *She left the room.* |

To express possession, belonging, or what something is made of in Spanish, the preposition **de** is used.

| | |
|---|---|
| Es la casa de mi tío. | *It is my uncle's house.* |
| El marido de mi hermana es tonto. | *My sister's husband is stupid.* |
| Quiero una taza de café. | *I want a cup of coffee.* |
| La pulsera es de plata. | *The bracelet is made of silver.* |
| Dale un vaso de vino. | *Give him a glass of wine.* |

To describe or identify someone or something by way of a characteristic or condition the preposition **de** is used. In English the preposition *"with"* is often used in these cases.

| | |
|---|---|
| La chica del pelo rubio es alta. | *The girl with the blonde hair is tall.* |
| Su novio es el chico del bigote. | *Her boyfriend is the boy with the moustache.* |
| La mujer del vestido rojo te mira. | *The woman in the red dress is looking at you.* |

English often uses a prepositional phrase beginning with *in* or *on* to talk about where someone or something is located. Spanish uses either **de** or a relative clause to express this idea. In these cases it is incorrect to use a prepositional phrase introduced by **en**.

| | |
|---|---|
| Mi amiga de la escuela me ayuda mucho. | *My friend at school helps me a lot.* |
| Los chicos de mi iglesia son amables. | *The boys at my church are nice.* |
| Los libros que están en la mesa son míos. | *The books on the table are mine.* |
| La casa que está en la esquina es bonita. | *The house on the corner is pretty.* |

As was true of **a**, the preposition **de** may be used in some cases to express the manner in which something is done.

| | |
|---|---|
| Lo aprendí de memoria. | *I learned it by memory.* |
| Lo hizo de mala gana. | *He did it unwillingly.* |
| De repente ella entró por la puerta. | *Suddenly she came through the door.* |

One of the most common ways to express the idea of *about* or *concerning* is to use the preposition **de**. In many cases, this will be equivalent to the expression **acerca de**.

| | |
|---|---|
| No quiero hablar de eso. | *I don't want to talk about that.* |
| Ellos no saben nada de mi trabajo. | *They don't know anything about my job.* |

In order to express a definite time of day in Spanish, the preposition **de** is used. If the time is not specific, the preposition **por** is used.

| | |
|---|---|
| La clase comienza a las ocho de la mañana. | *The class begins at eight in the morning.* |
| Siempre llegamos a las cuatro de la tarde. | *We always arrive at four in the afternoon.* |
| Ellos estudian por la mañana. | *They study in the morning.* |

| **Expressions with the Preposition De** | | | |
|---|---|---|---|
| abusar de | *to abuse, misuse* | olvidarse de | *to forget about* |
| acordarse de | *to remember* | quejarse de | *to complain about* |
| cambiar de | *to change* | reírse de | *to laugh at* |
| darse cuenta de | *to realize* | servir de | *to serve as* |
| depender de | *to depend on* | tratar de | *to try to* |
| enamorarse de | *to fall in love with* | | |

## Uses of En

When no motion is involved, the preposition **en** is used to indicate *in*, *on*, or *at* with expressions which refer to a specific location in time or space.

| | |
|---|---|
| Yo la vi en la fiesta. | *I saw her at the party.* |
| Ella está en su casa. | *She is at home.* |
| Nos conocimos en Cancún. | *We met in Cancun.* |
| En junio vamos a Madrid. | *In June we are going to Madrid.* |
| Dejé mis libros en la mesa. | *I left my books on the table.* |
| El cuadro está en la pared. | *The painting is on the wall.* |

Like **a** and **de**, the preposition **en** can be used to express manner or means of doing something. This use of **en** includes means or modes of transportation.

| | |
|---|---|
| Yo fui a México en avión. | *I went to Mexico by plane.* |
| Ella no hablaba en serio. | *She was not speaking seriously.* |
| Ellos intentaron en vano. | *They tried in vain.* |
| Lo dije en broma. | *I said it jokingly.* |
| No nos hablaron en inglés. | *They didn't speak to us in English.* |

**En** may also be used with units of time to express when something happens.

| | |
|---|---|
| En aquella época no había carros. | *At that time, there were no cars.* |
| Vamos a salir en dos horas. | *We are going to leave in two hours.* |
| En ese momento supimos la verdad. | *At that moment we found out the truth.* |

| **Expressions With the Preposition En** | | | |
|---|---|---|---|
| confiar en | *to trust, confide in* | influir en | *to influence* |
| consistir en | *to consist of* | pensar en | *to think about* |
| convertirse en | *to become* | quedar en | *to agree to, decide upon* |
| fijarse en | *to notice* | vacilar en | *to hesitate about* |

**Exercise 3.** Fill in the blank with the correct preposition, if needed.

1. Llegamos _____ cine a las siete.
2. Yo les mandé las fotos _____ mis padres.
3. La señora _____ la carnicería dice que no venden chuletas.
4. Ella nunca se ríe _____ mi hermano.
5. Yo trato _____ estudiar aquí, pero es imposible.
6. Este suéter está hecho _____ mano.
7. _____ aquellos días yo tenía mucho pelo.
8. Busco _____ mis llaves.
8. Yo la invité _____ salir, pero ella no quiso ir conmigo.
9. Tengo _____ dos hermanos. Ellos viven _____ casa.
10. Yo te hablaba _____ serio.
11. Ese chico se parece _____ su hermano.
12. _____ las seis comenzamos _____ jugar.
13. Ese chico siempre se queja _____ todo.
14. Me acordé _____ cerrar la puerta.
15. Acabo de llegar _____ tu casa.

**Exercise 4.** Fill in the blank with the correct preposition, if needed.

1. Ellos tienen que aprender _____ esquiar.
2. Son las nueve _____ la mañana.
3. Tenemos que esperar _____ el autobús.
4. _____ oír las malas noticias, todos se pusieron _____ llorar.
5. Ella tenía una habitación que daba _____ parque.
6. El reloj es _____ mi hermano.
7. Me fijé _____ el precio del anillo.
8. Me senté _____ mi computadora y comencé _____ trabajar.
9. Desafortunadamente, no puedo confiar _____ mis padres.
10. Les ayudé _____ construir la casa.

11. Vamos _____ esperar _____ Juan.

12. Dice que estaba enferma, pero sé que estaba _____ la playa.

13. La comida consistía _____ dos sándwiches y una manzana.

14. Llegué _____ aeropuerto muy tarde.

15. El hombre _____ la barba no pagó su cuenta.

**Exercise 5.** Translate the following sentences to Spanish.

1. We asked him for money.
_____

2. She trusts her boyfriend, but he has deceived her.
_____

3. He fell in love with her, but she rejected him.
_____

4. At that moment they began to look at the girl in the water.
_____

5. She changed clothes before going to her grandmother's house.
_____

6. When I saw them at school, they insisted on returning home with me.
_____

7. They agreed to sell us the house on the corner.
_____

8. While I was thinking about my trip to Cancún, a car ran over me.
_____

9. This house smells like roses.
_____

10. My cousins were laughing at the man in the car.
_____

## Uses of Por and Para

The prepositions **por** and **para** sometimes present a challenge for Spanish students. Part of the reason for this confusion has to do with the fact that each of these prepositions can be translated in many different ways in English. The fact that **por** and **para** can be translated using the same English preposition in some cases further complcates the situation.

| | |
|---|---|
| Camina por la playa. | *She is walking along the beach.* |
| Camina para la playa. | *She is walking towards the beach.* |
| | |
| Por su edad, juega muy bien. | *Because of his age he plays well.* |
| Para su edad, juega muy bien. | *He plays well for one his age.* |
| | |
| Voy a hacer la tarea para el lunes. | *I am going to do the homework by Monday.* |
| Vamos a viajar a Madrid por tren. | *We are going to travel to Madrid by train.* |
| | |
| El regalo es para ti. | *The gift is for you.* |
| Lo hice por ella. | *I did it for her (on her behalf).* |

Students trying to understand **por** and **para** often resort to memorizing lists of usages of the two prepositions. However, it is helpful to start with some generalizations about the basic meanings of these two prepositions. The most basic use of **para** involves destination or direction in time or space. It can be used to describe a physical destination, a goal, a recipient, or the time by which an action is to be completed. **Por** may be used to show movement through time or space as well as the motive or reasons for an action.

## Uses of Para

The preposition **para** is used to express destination or direction in time or space.

| | |
|---|---|
| Salgo para México mañana. | *I am leaving for Mexico tomorrow.* |
| Ahora estamos caminando para tu casa. | *We are walking towards your house.* |
| Tenemos que llegar para el viernes. | *We have to arrive by Friday.* |
| Ella estará aquí para el mes de noviembre. | *She will be here by the month of November.* |

It is not difficult to understand how the use of **para** is extended to describe a goal or the intended use of a particular item. In this sense **para** is being used to show suitability, purpose, goal, or use. **Para** can be used with an infinitive to express *in order to* or *to be about to do something*.

| | |
|---|---|
| Uso la escoba para barrer la cocina. | *I use the broom to sweep the kitchen.* |
| Este jarabe es muy bueno para la tos. | *This cough syrup is very good for a cough.* |
| Vine para ayudarte con la tarea. | *I came to help you with the homework.* |
| El dinero es para el taxi. | *The money is for the taxi.* |
| Vamos a la biblioteca para estudiar. | *We are going to the library (in order) to study.* |
| Necesito esta llave para abrir la puerta. | *I need this key to open the door.* |
| Estamos para salir. | *We are about to leave.* |

**Para** can also be used to show that some action or situation is out of the ordinary or unexpected under the circumstances.

| | |
|---|---|
| Para un niño de siete años, es muy alto. | *For a child of seven years, he is very tall.* |
| Para ser tan viejo, el coche cuesta mucho. | *In spite of its being so old, the car costs a lot.* |

In Spanish the preposition **para** is used to show that an opinion is being expressed.

| | |
|---|---|
| Para mí esta situación es muy complicada. | *In my opinion, this situation is very complicated.* |
| Para nosotros es una mala idea. | *In our opinion, it is a bad idea.* |

**Uses of Por**

**Por** can often be translated in English as *because of, on account of, on behalf of, in place of,* or *in favor of.*

| | |
|---|---|
| Yo llegué tarde por el tráfico. | *I arrived late because of the traffic.* |
| Ella va a hablar por ellos. | *She is going to speak for them (on their behalf).* |
| ¿Quieres trabajar por mí esta noche? | *Do you want to work in my place tonight?* |
| Estamos por el comercio libre. | *We are in favor of free trade.* |

When referring to location **por** shows movement along, by, or through a place. In this sense it is used to talk about location in a more general way.

| | |
|---|---|
| El hombre entró por la ventana. | *The man came in through the window.* |
| Caminamos por la calle. | *We walked along the street.* |
| El parque está por allí. | *The park is over there (in that general area).* |

With regard to expressions of time, **por** is again somewhat more vague than **a** or **de**. It is used for a period of time when no specific hour is mentioned.

| | |
|---|---|
| Nos quedamos allí por tres días. | *We stayed there for three days.* |
| Hablaron por mucho tiempo. | *They talked for a long time.* |
| Generalmente estudiamos por la tarde. | *We usually study in the afternoon.* |

To express the idea *in exchange for* or to talk about a rate or a mode of transportation, the preposition **por** is used.

| | |
|---|---|
| Lo vendí por veinte dólares. | *I sold it for twenty dollars.* |
| El carro viajaba a noventa millas por hora. | *The car was traveling ninety miles per hour.* |
| Preferimos ir a Francia por tren. | *We prefer to go to France by train.* |
| Ella gana treinta dólares por hora. | *She earns thirty dollars per hour.* |

**Por** is used before a noun which refers to the object of an errand.

| | |
|---|---|
| Ella va a la tienda por pan. | *She is going to the store for bread.* |
| Fui al supermercado por leche. | *I went to the supermarket for milk.* |

**Exercise 6.** Fill in the blank with either **por** or **para**.

1. Ella tiene un paquete_____mí.
2. Nosotros vamos al parque_____la tarde.
3. Ese hombre es demasiado viejo_____hacer eso.
4. Yo uso esto_____reparar el carro.
5. Pensamos estar allí_____un mes.
6. Salgo_____Europa mañana.
7. El banco está_____allí.
8. Ella no pudo ir_____la enfermedad de su mamá.
9. Yo trabajo cincuenta horas_____semana.
10. Fuimos al centro_____auto.
11. Cuando lo encontraron estaba caminando_____un barrio peligroso.
12. Ella no puede ir porque está enferma; voy_____ella.
13. _____ser tan viejo, tenía mucha experiencia con los caballos.
14. Entró en la casa_____la ventana de la calle.
15. Compramos los libros_____cincuenta dólares.

**Exercise 7.** Fill in the blank with either **por** or **para**.

1. Tuvimos que esperar_____dos horas_____entrar en el cine.
2. Habremos terminado la tarea_____el lunes.
3. Voy a votar_____el candidato honrado.
4. Es muy alto_____un niño de diez años.
5. Estoy mareada_____no haber comido.
6. Fui a la agencia_____mis boletos.
7. Cuando la llamamos, andaba_____California.
8. No va conmigo_____la tarea que tiene.
9. Tendremos todo preparado_____el viernes.
10. Nos gusta pasar_____las ruinas impresionantes.

# Conjunctions

Conjunctions are used to connect two or more elements of a sentence. These may include words to words, phrases to phrases, or clauses to clauses. The grammatical elements can either be of equal status in the sentence or the second may be subordinated to the first. If the two elements are of equal status, they are linked by a coordinating conjunction. If the second part of the sentence is subordinated to the first, a subordinating conjunction is used.

The coordinating conjunctions **y, o, ni, pero**, and **sino** are used to connect two equal parts of a sentence.

| | |
|---|---|
| Quiere ir, pero tiene que estudiar. | *She wants to go, but she has to study.* |
| Compré este libro y quiero leerlo. | *I bought this book and I want to read it.* |
| Ella no estudió francés sino inglés. | *She didn't study French but (instead) English.* |

Subordinating conjunctions introduce subordinate clauses. The most common subordinate conjunction is **que**. Others include **para que, sin que**, and **a fin de que**.

| | |
|---|---|
| Prefiero que te quedes aquí. | *I prefer that you stay here.* |
| Nos sentamos aquí para que nos vean. | *We are sitting here so that they will see us.* |

## Relationship of Adverbs, Prepositions, and Conjunctions

Many adverbs of place, sometimes referred to as locatives, have corresponding prepositional forms. Some nonlocative adverbs also have corresponding prepositions and/or conjunctions.

| | |
|---|---|
| Llamaron después que salimos. | *They called after we left.* |
| Vamos a hablar después. | *We are going to talk afterwards.* |
| Después de comer, vamos a hablar. | *After eating, we are going to talk.* |
| Hablamos después que salió mi abuela. | *We talked after my grandmother left.* |
| Lo botaron porque no trabajaba. | *They kicked him out because he didn't work.* |

Stanley Whitley (1986: 200) makes the very astute observation that this pattern deserves more pedagogical emphasis. He (1986: 201-02) makes this connection very clear by highlighting the parallel forms of some adverbs, prepositions, and conjunctions in Spanish and demonstrates that the locative adverbs are fairly consistent in that they add **de** for the corresponding preposition. Many nonlocatives have corresponding conjunctions which are formed by adding **que** to the adverb. The following charts are based on Whitley's comparisons.

**Locatives**

| | | |
|---|---|---|
| afuera | *outside* | adverb |
| fuera de | *outside of* | preposition |
| | | |
| cerca | *nearby, close by* | adverb |
| cerca de | *close to* | preposition |
| | | |
| enfrente | *in front* | adverb |
| enfrente de | *in front of* | preposition |
| | | |
| lejos | *far, far away* | adverb |
| lejos de | *far from* | preposition |

**Nonlocatives**

| | | |
|---|---|---|
| además | *besides, in addition* | adverb |
| además de | *besides, in addition to* | preposition |
| además de que | *besides, in addition to* | conjunction |
| | | |
| antes | *beforehand* | adverb |
| antes de | *before* | preposition |
| antes de que | *before* | conjunction |
| | | |
| después | *afterwards* | adverb |
| después de | *after* | preposition |
| después que | *after* | conjunction |
| | | |
| por eso | *so, therefore* | adverb |
| por | *because of* | preposition |
| porque | *because* | conjunction |

    Errors such those shown below occur because students do not grasp the basic function of each of these grammatical categories. Adverbs are used intransitively (without an object), while prepositions can take a noun phrase object or an infinitive object. Conjunctions are used to connect words, phrases, clauses, or sentences. By understanding this relationship and knowing the grammatical function of each of these, students can avoid errors such as those exemplified in the following sentences.

| | | |
|---|---|---|
| *Llegamos tarde porque de la lluvia.<br>Llegamos tarde por la lluvia. | *We arrived late because of the rain.* | (incorrect)<br>(correct) |
| *Llamé a mi mamá antes de.<br>Llamé a mi mamá antes. | *I called my mom beforehand.* | (incorrect)<br>(correct) |
| *Después la película, fuimos a comer.<br>Después de la película, fuimos a comer. | *After the movie, we went to eat.* | (incorrect)<br>(correct) |
| *Ellos esperaron hasta llegué.<br>Ellos esperaron hasta que llegué. | *They waited until I arrived.* | (incorrect)<br>(correct) |

**Exercise 8.** Fill in the blank with the correct adverb, preposition, or conjunction.

1. Los niños están jugando_____.  (outside)
2. Voy al cine_____salga mi jefe.  (after)
3. Mi casa está_____la ciudad.  (far from)
4. _____estudiar tanto, la pobre chica tiene que trabajar.  (Besides)
5. Estoy seguro que el restaurante está_____.  (nearby)
6. Ella cantó_____todos se pusieron a gritar.  (until)
7. No, te dije que íbamos a comer_____.  (before)
8. Mi casa está_____la suya.  (beside)
9. No podemos verla_____el martes.  (until)
10. La comida no estaba lista; _____, tuvimos que esperar.  (So)
11. Ella se queda en casa_____ser perezosa.  (because of)
12. Trabajamos_____tú puedas comer bien.  (so)
13. ¿No dijiste que vivías_____la universidad?  (near)
14. ¿Quieres ir a un restaurante_____cocinar.  (instead of)
15. No saca buenas notas _____es flojo.  (since)

# CHAPTER 11

# Nonfinites and Reverse Constructions

Both Spanish and English have a class of verb forms sometimes referred to as *nonfinites*. These constructions are not inflected for person, number, tense, or mood. However, nonfinites may function as nouns, adjectives, or adverbs. In Spanish the three types of nonfinites are infinitives, gerunds, and present participles.

The terms gerund and present participle are used in different ways in Spanish and English. Whitley notes (1986:93) that "what is called a gerund in English may not necessarily match an English or Latin one." Furthermore, there is much variation in how these terms are used even with regard to Spanish grammar. In this chapter, I shall attempt to use the term present participle in reference to the forms used with the progressive tenses and the term gerund elsewhere.

## The Infinitive

As you already know, the infinitive is the typical citation form of the verb used in dictionaries. For purposes of conjugation, Spanish verbs are grouped according to the ending of the infinitives. The infinitive in Spanish can function as a noun, a direct object, or the object of a preposition.

### The Infinitive as a Noun

In Spanish the infinitive may serve as the subject of a sentence. The infinitive used as a subject occurs most often in sentence-initial position. As it is being used as a noun in this case, it may or may not take a definite article. This usage very often corresponds to the English gerund.

| | |
|---|---|
| (El) estudiar es necesario. | *Studying is necessary.* |
| (El) viajar es divertido. | *Traveling is fun.* |
| (El) comer bien es esencial. | *Eating well is essential.* |
| (El) ver es creer. | *Seeing is believing.* |

When used as a noun, the infinitive sometimes follows an adjective. In these cases, the noun still retains its function as the subject of the sentence.

| | |
|---|---|
| Es importante llegar temprano. | *It is important to arrive early.* |
| Es imposible dormir aquí. | *It is impossible to sleep here.* |

## The Infinitive Used After Prepositions

If the person performing the action referred to by an infinitive is also the subject of the sentence, the infinitive functions as the object of that verb. Most verbs do not require a preposition before the infinitive.

| | |
|---|---|
| Quiero ir mañana. | *I want to go tomorrow.* |
| Ellos necesitan salir temprano. | *They need to leave early.* |
| Ella puede mirar la película. | *She can watch the movie.* |

However, there are some verbs that do require that a preposition be used before an infinitive. While they must be learned on a case-by-case basis for the most part, the majority of these verbs will take the prepositions **a**, **de**, **en** or **con**.

---

**Verbs Requiring Prepositions Before Infinitives**

**a**

| | |
|---|---|
| aprender a | *to learn to* |
| atreverse a | *to dare to* |
| ayudar a | *to help to* |
| comenzar a | *to begin to* |
| empezar a | *to begin to* |
| enseñar a | *to teach to* |
| invitar a | *to invite to* |
| ponerse a | *to begin to* |
| volver a | *to do again* |

**de**

| | |
|---|---|
| acabar de | *to finish* |
| acordarse de | *to remember* |
| alegrarse de | *to be glad of* |
| cansarse de | *to get tired of* |
| olvidarse de | *to forget about* |
| tratar de | *to try to* |

**en**

| | |
|---|---|
| consentir en | *to agree to* |
| consistir en | *to consist of* |
| insistir en | *to insist on* |
| pensar en | *to think about* |
| persistir en | *to persist in* |
| tardar en | *to delay in* |

**con**

| | |
|---|---|
| contar con | *to count on* |
| soñar con | *to dream about* |

---

| | |
|---|---|
| Ella comienza a trabajar. | *She is beginning to work.* |
| Ellos se cansan de estudiar. | *They are getting tired of studying.* |
| Nosotros tardamos en llegar. | *We were late in arriving.* |
| Sueño con vivir en España. | *I am dreaming about living in Spain.* |

## Infinitives without a Change of Subject

When there is no change of subject, the infinitive may also be used after some prepositions in order to indicate time, manner, or purpose. The infinitive becomes part of a prepositional phrase which functions as an adverb. In English, the gerund is often used to express this idea.

| | |
|---|---|
| Trabajamos para ganar dinero. | *We work in order to earn money.* |
| Ellos comieron antes de salir. | *They ate before leaving.* |
| Todos salieron sin hablar. | *Everyone left without talking.* |
| Van a comer despúes de mirar el partido. | *They are going to eat after watching the game.* |

## Al + Infinitive

The infinitive is used in the construction **al + infinitive** where English uses the construction **upon + gerund**.

Al llegar a clase, los estudiantes se pusieron a estudiar.
*Upon arriving to class, the students began to study.*

Al oír las noticias, Juan decidió salir inmediatamente.
*Upon hearing the news, Juan decided to leave immediately.*

## Adjective + Infinitive

The infinitive may be used in the construction (**ser + adjective + de**) to express ideas such as the following.

| | |
|---|---|
| El español es fácil de aprender. | *Spanish is easy to learn.* |
| Esa canción es imposible de olvidar. | *That song is impossible to forget.* |
| El sabor es difícil de describir. | *The flavor is difficult to describe.* |

## Other Uses of the Infinitive

The infinitive can be used as a command. This use of the infinitive with imperative force is most often seen in public settings, on street signs, etc.

| | |
|---|---|
| No fumar. | *No smoking.* |
| No estacionar. | *No parking.* |

The infinitive may be used with verbs of perception such as **oír** and **ver**, in order to indicate that an action has been completed.

| | |
|---|---|
| La vio salir. | *He saw her go out.* |
| Te oí cantar. | *I heard you singing.* |

## The Present Participle and Gerund

As shown in Chapter 1, the present participle/gerund in Spanish is formed by removing the infinitive endings from the verb and adding **-ando** for **-ar** verbs and **-iendo** for **-er** and **-ir** verbs. The most common use of the present participle is with the progressive tenses.

Ella está hablando por teléfono. *She is talking on the phone.*
María estaba durmiendo cuando la vi. *María was sleeping when I saw her.*

In English and Spanish, the gerund may function as an adverb by indicating time, manner, purpose, reason or condition. In some cases, this usage is exactly equivalent to using the English present participle as an adverb that modifies another verb.

Los chicos salieron corriendo. *The boys left running.*
Ella entró llorando. *She came in crying.*

However, it is important to remember that the gerund (present participle) cannot be used as an adjective in Spanish. In these cases, Spanish would use an adjective clause.

El hombre se quejó del perro que ladraba.
*The man complained about the barking dog.*

El chico que juega en el jardín es mi sobrino.
*The boy playing in the garden is my nephew.*

While **estar** is the verb which is most often used with the present participle to indicate progressive action, other verbs may also be used to emphasize different aspects of an ongoing action. Perhaps the most common of these are the verbs **andar**, **seguir**, **ir**, and **venir**. The verb **andar** is used to indicate *wandering around* or *going around*, with the idea that the action is somewhat random or unplanned.

As Solé and Solé (165: 46-47) point out, both **ir** and **venir** retain their basic sense of movement toward or away from, respectively. For this reason, **ir** may be used with adverbs of degree, manner, or comparison to indicate the gradual forward progression in time of an action. The verb **venir** may be used with temporal expressions such as **hace .... que**, **desde**, and **desde hace** to emphasize that an action began in the past and has gradually continued into the present. When used in this way, **venir** may indicate the speaker's irritation about the situation described. The verb **seguir** is often used to stress the habitual or ongoing nature of an action.

Esos chicos andan buscando problemas.
*Those boys go around looking for trouble.*

Poco a poco la situación va mejorando.
*Little by little the situation is improving.*

Hace dos años que viene diciendo lo mismo.
*He has been saying that for two years.*

A pesar de su edad, mi papá sigue cortando el césped todos los días.
*In spite of his age, my dad continues mowing the yard every day.*

In some Spanish sentences, the gerund is used in a way that would be best translated in English as (**by + gerund**) or (**while + gerund**).

Trabajando quince horas al día, Javier pudo ganar el dinero.
*By working fifteen hours a day, Javier was able to earn the money.*

Hablando con su mamá, Ana decidió que necesitaba quedarse en casa.
*While talking with her mother, Ana decided that she needed to stay home.*

Diciendo mentiras, vas a perder a todos tus amigos.
*By telling lies, you are going to lose all your friends.*

In English the gerund is often used as a noun, particularly at the beginning of a sentence. Remember that it is the infinitive, not the gerund, which functions as a noun in Spanish.

| | |
|---|---|
| (El) nadar es divertido. | *Swimming is fun.* |
| (El) leer es importante. | *Reading is important.* |

**Exercise 1.** Translate the following sentences to Spanish.

1. By sending the package early, we will save money.
   _____

2. Running is good for your health.
   _____

3. Upon discovering the error, she immediately called her boss.
   _____

4. I saw them talking in the hallway.
   _____

5. The screaming child was annoying everyone in the movie theater.
   _____

6. She heard us leave.
   _____

7. He always went around telling lies.

8. They wanted to get out of the burning building.

9. That man is hard to understand.

10. She keeps on asking if we are going to get married.

**Exercise 2.** Translate the following sentences to Spanish.

1. Living here is not going to be easy for us.

2. We used to like walking through the forest.

3. She tried to grab one of the falling leaves.

4. He left without giving us his address.

5. We are going to talk with them before leaving.

6. While living with her mother-in-law, she learned to cook.

7. She began reading the book to her son.

8. He saw them pick up the trash.

9. They are thinking about leaving early.

10. The prices here keep going up.

## Gustar and Reverse Constructions

**The Verb Gustar**

The most common way to express the English verb *to like* in Spanish is to use the verb **gustar**. However, it may be helpful for students to think of the verb **gustar** as *to be pleasing to* rather than *to like*, as **gustar** functions differently from its English counterpart. In **gustar** constructions the subject of the English sentence becomes the indirect object of the Spanish sentence. The direct object of the English sentence is the subject of the Spanish sentence.

Even more confusing for English-speaking students is the fact that the subject is generally placed at the end of the sentence in Spanish. As always, the verb agrees with the subject of the sentence and not with the indirect object. Because English and Spanish have opposite word order in this case, verbs like **gustar** are sometimes referred to as *reverse constructions*.

**English**

| They | like | the class. |
|---|---|---|
| subject | verb | direct object |

**Spanish**

| Les | gusta | la clase. |
|---|---|---|
| indirect object | verb | subject |

Because the person doing the liking is always an indirect object in the Spanish construction, the verb **gustar** will always be preceded by an indirect object pronoun in Spanish. The indirect object may be reinforced or clarified by a prepositional phrase which is introduced by the preposition **a**. This is especially true of the third-person singular and plural forms **le** and **les**. If the sentence is negative, the **no** must precede the indirect object pronoun. The prepositional phrase may be placed at the beginning or at the end of the sentence.

| Les gustó la película a ellos. | *They liked the movie.* |
|---|---|
| Le gustan los perros a ella. | *She likes dogs.* |
| A mí me gustan los parques. | *I like parks.* |
| A Mary no le gustan los gatos. | *Mary doesn't like cats.* |
| No nos gustan esas fotos. | *We don't like those pictures.* |
| Le gustan los postres a mi hermano. | *My brother likes desserts.* |

When one talks about liking to do something, the infinitive functions as the subject of **gustar**. In this case, the verb **gustar** will always be in the third-person singular form regardless of how many infinitives are being used.

| A mis primos les gusta cantar. | *My cousins like to sing.* |
|---|---|
| Me gusta leer, escribir, y hablar. | *I like to read, write, and talk.* |

| Constructions with Gustar | | | |
|---|---|---|---|
| **Prepositional Pronoun** (Optional) | **Indirect Object Pronoun** (Person Liking) | **Form of Gustar** (3rd Person Singular or 3rd Person Plural) | **Subject** (What is liked) |
| a mí | me | | |
| a ti | te | | |
| a él, a ella, a usted | le | | |
| | | gusta | singular noun or infinitive(s) |
| | | gustan | plural noun |
| a nosotros(as) | nos | | |
| a vosotros(as) | os | | |
| a ellos, a ellas, a ustedes | les | | |

One common error involves the use of a direct object pronoun in **gustar** constructions that do not have an overt subject. This is understandable since the equivalent English construction does have a direct object pronoun. However, in this case *it* functions as the subject of the sentence in Spanish. Spanish does not use a subject pronoun to express *it* when referring to inanimate objects.

| | |
|---|---|
| Te gusta la comida. | *Do you like the food?* |
| Sí, me gusta. | *Yes, I like it.* |
| *Sí, me lo gusta. | (incorrect) |
| | |
| ¿Le gustan los pantalones a Juan? | *Does Juan like the pants?* |
| Sí, le gustan. | *Yes, he likes them.* |
| *Sí, se los gustan. | (incorrect) |

### Other Reverse Construction Verbs

Although the verb **gustar** is the most common example of the reverse construction, it is by no means the only one. There are many other very common verbs which behave in the same way as **gustar**.

| | |
|---|---|
| Me duelen las piernas. | *My feet are hurting.* |
| No les importaba el ambiente. | *They didn't care about the environment.* |
| Nos encanta bailar. | *We love to dance.* |
| Les faltan dos mantas. | *They need (are lacking) two blankets.* |
| Me quedan seis dólares. | *I have six dollars left.* |
| ¿Te molestaba el ruido? | *Was the noise bothering you?* |

| Reverse Construction Verbs | | | |
|---|---|---|---|
| caer bien/mal | to like, dislike (people) | importar | to matter, care about |
| doler | to hurt | interesar | to interest |
| encantar | to love (not people) | molestar | to bother |
| faltar | to lack | quedar | to have left |

**Exercise 3.** Translate the following sentences to Spanish.

1. They have ten forks left, but they need four spoons (don't use **necesitar**).

2. I don't like her. She always goes around complaining.

3. They love this place, but I dream about my house at the beach.

4. It doesn't matter to me that they smoke.

5. Her head hurts, but she doesn't want to take an aspirin.

6. We saw a horror movie last night. It scared us, but we liked it a lot.

7. Working is very hard for her, but she needs the money.

8. I am interested in psychology. I want to take some courses before graduating.

9. She would like to leave, but they keep giving her more money.

10. This problem is hard to resolve.

**Exercise 4.** Translate the following sentences to Spanish.

1. Since they had not arrived on time, they had to sit near the exit.

2. We didn't tell you because of your recent accident.

3. Because the policeman gave me a ticket, my dad took away my keys.

4. That possibility is hard to accept.

5. They are traveling to that region in September.

6. Do you like these earrings? I don't like them.

7. Talking is easy, but what we need is action.

8. They needed you to teach them to swim.

9. I know that they were here until 9:00 because they were making so much noise.

10. We used to love walking in this neighborhood at night.

# *APPENDIX I*

# Verb Conjugations

## Regular Verb Conjugations

### Regular –AR Verb Conjugations

| | |
|---|---|
| Present ind. | hablo, hablas, habla, hablamos, habláis, hablan |
| Preterit | hablé, hablaste, habló, hablamos, hablasteis, hablaron |
| Imperfect ind. | hablaba, hablabas, hablaba, hablábamos, hablabais, hablaban |
| Future | hablaré, hablarás, hablará, hablaremos, hablaréis, hablarán |
| Conditional | hablaría, hablarías, hablaría, hablaríamos, hablaríais, hablarían |
| Present perfect Indicative | he hablado, has hablado, ha hablado, hemos hablado, habéis hablado, han hablado |
| Past perfect indicative | había hablado, habías hablado, había hablado, habíamos hablado, habíais hablado, habían hablado |
| Future perfect indicative | habré hablado, habrás hablado, habrá hablado, habremos hablado, habréis hablado, habrán hablado |
| Conditional perfect indicative | habría hablado, habrías hablado, habría hablado, habríamos hablado, habríais hablado, habrían hablado |
| Present subj. | hable, hables, hable, hablemos, habléis, hablen |
| Imperfect subj. | hablara, hablaras, hablara, habláramos, hablarais, hablaran |
| Present perfect subjunctive | haya hablado, hayas hablado, haya hablado, hayamos hablado, hayáis hablado, hayan hablado |
| Past perfect subjunctive | hubiera hablado, hubieras hablado, hubiera hablado, hubiéramos hablado, hubierais hablado, hubieran hablado |

| | |
|---|---|
| Tú imperative | habla no hables |
| Vosotros imp. | hablad no habléis |
| Usted imp. | hable no hable |
| Ustedes imp. | hablen no hablen |
| Present part. | hablando |

**Regular -ER Verb Conjugations**

| | |
|---|---|
| Present ind. | como, comes, come, comemos, coméis, comen |
| Preterit | comí, comiste, comió, comimos, comisteis, comieron |
| Imperfect ind. | comía, comías, comía, comíamos, comíais, comían |
| Future | comeré, comerás, comerá, comeremos, comeréis, comerán |
| Conditional | comería, comerías, comería, comeríamos, comeríais, comerían |
| Present perfect indicative | he comido, has comido, ha comido, hemos comido, habéis comido, han comido |
| Past perfect indicative | había comido, habías comido, había comido, habíamos comido, habíais comido, habían comido |
| Future perfect indicative | habré comido, habrás comido, habrá comido, habremos comido, habréis comido, habrán comido |
| Conditional perfect ind. | habría comido, habrías comido, habría comido, habríamos comido, habríais comido, habrían comido |
| Present subj. | coma, comas, coma, comamos, comáis, coman |
| Imperfect subj. | comiera, comieras, comiera, comiéramos, comierais, comieran |
| Present perfect subjunctive | haya comido, hayas comido, haya comido, hayamos comido, hayáis comido, hayan comido |
| Past perfect subjunctive | hubiera comido, hubieras comido, hubiera comido, hubiéramos comido, hubierais comido, hubieran comido |
| Tú imperative | come no comas |
| Vosotros imp. | comed no comáis |

| | |
|---|---|
| Usted imp. | coma no coma |
| Ustedes imp. | coman no coman |
| Present part. | comiendo |

## Regular -IR Verb Conjugations

| | |
|---|---|
| Present ind. | vivo, vives, vive, vivimos, vivís, viven |
| Preterit | viví, viviste, vivió, vivimos, vivisteis, vivieron |
| Imperfect ind. | vivía, vivías, vivía, vivíamos, vivíais, vivían |
| Future | viviré, vivirás, vivirá, viviremos, viviréis, vivirán |
| Conditional | viviría, vivirías, viviría, viviríamos, viviríais, vivirían |
| Present perfect indicative | he vivido, has vivido, ha vivido, hemos vivido, habéis vivido, han vivido |
| Past perfect indicative | había vivido, habías vivido, había vivido, habíamos vivido, habíais vivido, habían vivido |
| Future perfect indicative | habré vivido, habrás vivido, habrá vivido, habremos vivido, habréis vivido, habrán vivido |
| Conditional perfect indicative | habría vivido, habrías vivido, habría vivido, habríamos vivido, habríais vivido, habrían vivido |
| Present subj. | viva, vivas, viva, vivamos, viváis, vivan |
| Imperfect subj. | viviera, vivieras, viviera, viviéramos, vivierais, vivieran |
| Present perfect subjunctive | haya vivido, hayas vivido, haya vivido, hayamos vivido, hayáis vivido, hayan vivido |
| Past perfect subjunctive | hubiera vivido, hubieras vivido, hubiera vivido, hubiéramos vivido, hubierais vivido, hubieran vivido |
| Tú imperative | vive no vivas |
| Vosotros imp. | vivid no viváis |
| Usted imp. | viva no viva |

| | |
|---|---|
| Ustedes imp. | vivan no vivan |
| Present part. | viviendo |

## Spelling-Change Verbs

### buscar-to look for (c to qu)

| | |
|---|---|
| Preterit | busqué, buscaste, buscó, buscamos, buscasteis, buscaron |
| Present subj. | busque, busques, busque, busquemos, busquéis, busquen |
| Tú imp. | busca no busques |
| Vosotros imp. | buscad no busquéis |
| Usted imp. | busque no busque |
| Ustedes imp. | busquen no busquen |

### llegar-to arrive (g to gu)

| | |
|---|---|
| Preterit | llegué, llegaste, llegó, llegamos, llegasteis, llegaron |
| Present subj. | llegue, llegues, llegue, lleguemos, lleguéis, lleguen |
| Tú imp. | llega no llegues |
| Vosotros imp. | llegad no lleguéis |
| Usted imp. | llegue no llegue |
| Ustedes imp. | lleguen no lleguen |

### comenzar-to begin (z to c)

| | |
|---|---|
| Preterit | comencé, comenzaste, comenzó, comenzamos, comenzasteis, comenzaron |
| Present subj. | comience, comiences, comience, comencemos, comencéis, comiencen |
| Tú imp. | comienza no comiences |
| Vosotros imp. | comenzad no comencéis |
| Usted imp. | comience no comience |
| Ustedes imp. | comiencen no comiencen |

### escoger-to choose (g to j)

| | |
|---|---|
| Present ind. | escojo, escoges, escoge, escogemos, escogéis, escogen |
| Present subj. | escoja, escojas, escoja, escojamos, escojáis, escojan |
| Tú imp. | escoge no escojas |
| Vosotros imp. | escoged no escojáis |
| Usted imp. | escoja no escoja |
| Ustedes imp. | escojan no escojan |

### convencer-to convince (c to z)

| | |
|---|---|
| Present ind. | convenzo, convences, convence, convencemos, convencéis, convencen |
| Present subj. | convenza, convenzas, convenza, convenzamos, convenzáis, convenzan |
| Tú imp. | convence no convenzas |
| Vosotros imp. | convenced no convenzáis |
| Usted imp. | convenza no convenza |
| Ustedes imp. | convenzan no convenzan |

### conocer-to know, be familiar with (c to zc)

| | |
|---|---|
| Present ind. | conozco, conoces, conoce, conocemos, conocéis, conocen |
| Present subj. | conozca, conozcas, conozca, conozcamos, conozcáis, conozcan |
| Tú imp. | conoce no conozcas |
| Vosotros imp. | conoced no conozcáis |
| Usted imp. | conozca no conozca |
| Ustedes imp. | conozcan no conozcan |

### seguir-to continue, follow (gu to g)

| | |
|---|---|
| Present ind. | sigo, sigues, sigue, seguimos, seguís, siguen |

| | |
|---|---|
| Present subj. | siga, sigas, siga, sigamos, sigáis, sigan |
| Tú imp. | sigue no sigas |
| Vosotros imp. | seguid no sigáis |
| Usted imp. | siga no siga |
| Ustedes imp. | sigan no sigan |

### construir-to build (i to y) (-uir verbs)

| | |
|---|---|
| Present ind. | construye, construyes, construye, construimos, construís, construyen |
| Preterit | construí, construiste, construyó, construimos, construisteis, construyeron |
| Present subj. | construya, construyas, construya, construyamos, construyáis, construyan |
| Tú imp. | construye no construyas |
| Vosotros imp. | construid no construyáis |
| Usted imp. | construya no construya |
| Ustedes imp. | construyan no construyan |
| Present part. | construyendo |

### leer-to read(i to y) (-eer verbs)

| | |
|---|---|
| Preterit | leí, leíste, leyó, leímos, leísteis, leyeron |
| Imperfect subj. | leyera, leyeras, leyera, leyéramos, leyerais, leyeran |
| Present part. | leyendo |

### continuar-to continue (u to ú)

| | |
|---|---|
| Present ind. | continúo, continúas, continúa, continuamos, continuáis, continúan |
| Present subj. | continúe, continúes, continúe, continuemos, continuéis, continúen |
| Tú imp. | continúa no continúes |
| Vosotros imp. | continuad no continuéis |

| | |
|---|---|
| Usted imp. | continúe no continúe |
| Ustedes imp. | continúen no continúen |

### enviar-to send (i to í)

| | |
|---|---|
| Present ind. | envío, envías, envía, enviamos, enviáis, envían |
| Present subj. | envíe, envíes, envíe, enviemos, enviéis, envíen |
| Tú imp. | envía no envíes |
| Vosotros imp. | enviad no enviéis |
| Usted imp. | envíe no envíe |
| Ustedes imp. | envíen no envíen |

# Irregular Verb Conjugations

## Stem-Changing Verbs

### -AR Stem Changing Verbs: cerrar-to close (e to ie)

| | |
|---|---|
| Present ind. | cierro, cierras, cierra, cerramos, cerráis, cierran |
| Present subj. | cierre, cierres, cierre, cerremos, cerréis, cierren |
| Tú imp. | cierra no cierres |
| Vosotros imp. | cerrad no cerréis |
| Usted imp. | cierre no cierre |
| Ustedes imp. | cierren no cierren |

### -ER Stem-Changing Verbs: volver-to return (o to ue)

| | |
|---|---|
| Present ind. | vuelvo, vuelves, vuelve, volvemos, volvéis, vuelven |
| Present subj. | vuelvo, vuelvas, vuelva, volvamos, volváis, vuelvan |
| Tú imp. | vuelve no vuelvas |
| Vosotros imp. | volved no volváis |

| | |
|---|---|
| Usted imp. | vuelva no vuelva |
| Ustedes imp. | vuelvan no vuelvan |

## -IR Stem-Changing Verbs: sentir-to feel (e to i)

| | |
|---|---|
| Present ind. | pido, pides, pide, pedimos, pedís, piden |
| Preterit | pedí, pediste, pidió, pedimos, pedisteis, pidieron |
| Present subj. | pida, pidas, pida, pidamos, pidáis, pidan |
| Imperfect subj. | pidiera, pidieras, pidiera, pidiéramos, pidierais, pidieran |
| Tú imp. | pide no pidas |
| Vosotros imp. | pedid no pidáis |
| Present part. | pidiendo |

## -IR Stem-Changing Verbs: dormir-to sleep (o to u)

| | |
|---|---|
| Present ind. | duermo, duermes, duerme, dormimos, dormís, duermen |
| Preterit | dormí, dormiste, durmió, dormimos, dormisteis, durmieron |
| Present subj. | duerma, duermas, duerma, durmamos, durmáis, duerman |
| Imperfect subj. | durmiera, durmieras, durmiera, durmiéramos, durmierais, durmieran |
| Tú imp. | duerme no duermas |
| Vosotros imp. | dormid no durmáis |
| Usted imp. | duerma no duerma |
| Ustedes imp. | duerman no duerman |
| Present part. | durmiendo |

## Common Irregular Verbs

### andar-to walk

| | |
|---|---|
| Preterit | anduve, anduviste, anduvo, anduvimos, anduvisteis, anduvieron |
| Imperfect subj. | anduviera, anduvieras, anduviera, anduviéramos, anduvierais, anduvieran |

### caer-to fall

| | |
|---|---|
| Present ind. | caigo, caes, cae, caemos, caéis, caen |
| Preterit | caí, caíste, cayó, caímos, caísteis, cayeron |
| Present subj. | caiga, caigas, caiga, caigamos, caigáis, caigan |
| Imperfect subj. | cayera, cayeras cayera, cayéramos, cayerais, cayeran |
| Present part. | cayendo |
| Past part. | caído |

### conducir-to drive

| | |
|---|---|
| Present ind. | conduzco, conduces, conduce, conducimos, conducís, conducen |
| Preterit | conduje, condujiste, condujo, condujimos, condujisteis, condujeron |
| Present subj. | conduzca, conduzca, conduzca, conduzcamos, conduzcáis, conduzcan |
| Imperfect subjunctive | condujera, condujeras, condujera, condujéramos, condujerais, condujeran |

### dar-to give

| | |
|---|---|
| Present ind. | doy, das, da, damos, dais, dan |
| Preterit | di, diste, dio, dimos, disteis, dieron |
| Present subj. | dé, des, dé, demos, deis, den |
| Imperfect subj. | diera, dieras, diera, diéramos, dierais, dieran |

### decir-to say, tell

| | |
|---|---|
| Present ind. | digo, dices, dice, decimos, decís, dicen |
| Preterit | dije, dijiste, dijo, dijimos, dijisteis, dijeron |
| Future | diré, dirás, dirá, diremos, diréis, dirán |

| | |
|---|---|
| Condtional | diría, dirías, diría, diríamos, diríais, dirían |
| Present subj. | diga, digas, diga, digamos, digáis, digan |
| Imperfect subj. | dijera, dijeras, dijera, dijéramos, dijerais, dijeran |
| Present part. | diciendo |
| Past part. | dicho |
| Tú imperative | di |

**estar-to be**

| | |
|---|---|
| Present ind. | estoy, estás, está, estamos, estáis, están |
| Preterit | estuve, estuviste, estuvo, estuvimos, estuvisteis, estuvieron |
| Present subj. | esté, estés, esté, estemos, estéis, estén |
| Imperfect subj. | estuviera, estuvieras, estuviera, estuviéramos, estuvierais, estuvieran |

**haber-to have**

| | |
|---|---|
| Present ind. | he, has, ha, hemos, habéis, han |
| Preterit | hube, hubiste, hubo, hubimos, hubisteis, hubieron |
| Future | habré, habrás, habrá, habremos, habréis, habrán |
| Condtional | habría, habrías, habría, habríamos, habríais, habrían |
| Present subj. | haya, hayas, haya, hayamos, hayáis, hayan |
| Imperfect subj. | hubiera, hubieras, hubiera, hubiéramos, hubierais, hubieran |

**hacer-to do, make**

| | |
|---|---|
| Present ind. | hago, haces, hace, hacemos, hacéis, hacen |
| Preterit | hice, hiciste, hizo, hicimos, hicisteis, hicieron |
| Future | haré, harás, hará, haremos, haréis, harán |
| Condtional | haría, harías, haría, haríamos, haríais, harían |

| | |
|---|---|
| Present subj. | haga, hagas, haga, hagamos, hagáis, hagan |
| Imperfect subj. | hiciera, hicieras, hiciera, hiciéramos, hicierais, hicieron |
| Past part. | hecho |
| Tú imperative | haz |

**ir-to go**

| | |
|---|---|
| Present ind. | voy, vas, va, vamos, vais, van |
| Preterit | fui, fuiste, fue, fuimos, fuisteis, fueron |
| Imperfect ind. | iba, ibas, iba, íbamos, ibais, iban |
| Present subj. | vaya, vayas, vaya, vayamos, vayáis, vayan |
| Imperfect subj. | fuera, fueras, fuera, fuéramos, fuerais, fueran |
| Present part. | yendo |
| Tú imperative | Ve |

**oír-to hear**

| | |
|---|---|
| Present ind. | oigo, oyes, oye, oímos, oís, oyen |
| Preterit | oí, oíste, oyó, oímos, oísteis, oyeron |
| Present subj. | oiga, oigas, oiga, oigamos, oigáis, oigan |
| Imperfect subj. | oyera, oyeras, oyera, oyéramos, oyerais, oyeran |
| Present part. | oyendo |

**poder-can, to be able to**

| | |
|---|---|
| Present ind. | puedo, puedes, puede, podemos, podéis, pueden |
| Preterit | pude, pudiste, pudo, pudimos, pudisteis, pudieron |
| Future | podré, podrás, podrá, podremos, podréis, podrán |
| Condtional | podría, podrías, podría, podríamos, podríais, podrían |
| Present subj. | pueda, puedas, pueda, podamos, podáis, puedan |

| | |
|---|---|
| Imperfect subj. | pudiera, pudieras, pudiera, pudiéramos, pudierais, pudieran |
| Present part. | pudiendo |

### poner-to put, place

| | |
|---|---|
| Present ind. | pongo, pones, pone, ponemos, ponéis, ponen |
| Preterit | puse, pusiste, puso, pusimos, pusisteis, pusieron |
| Future | pondré, pondrás, pondrá, pondremos, pondréis, pondrán |
| Condtional | pondría, pondrías, pondría, pondríamos, pondríais, pondrían |
| Present subj. | ponga, pongas, ponga, pongamos, pongáis, pongan |
| Imperfect subj. | pusiera, pusieras, pusiera, pusiéramos, pusierais, pusieran |
| Past part. | puesto |

### querer-to want

| | |
|---|---|
| Present ind. | quiero, quieres, quiere, queremos, queréis, quieren |
| Preterit | quise, quisiste, quiso, quisimos, quisisteis, quisieron |
| Future | querré, querrás, querrá, querremos, querréis, querrán |
| Condtional | querría, querrías, querría, querríamos, querríais, querrían |
| Present subj. | quiera, quieras, quiera, queramos, queráis, quieran |
| Imperfect subj. | quisiera, quisieras, quisiera, quisiéramos, quisierais, quisieran |

### saber-to know

| | |
|---|---|
| Present ind. | sé, sabes, sabe, sabemos, sabéis, saben |
| Preterit | supe, supiste, supo, supimos, supisteis, supieron |
| Future | sabré, sabrás, sabrá, sabremos, sabréis, sabrán |
| Condtional | sabría, sabrías, sabría, sabríamos, sabríais, sabrían |
| Present subj. | sepa, sepas, sepa, sepamos, sepáis, sepan |
| Imperfect subj. | supiera, supieras, supiera, supiéramos, supierais, supieran |

### salir-to go out, leave

| | |
|---|---|
| Present ind. | salgo, sales, sale, salimos, salís, salen |
| Future | saldré, saldrás, saldrá, saldremos, saldréis, saldrán |
| Condtional | saldría, saldrías, saldría, saldríamos, saldríais, saldrían |
| Present subj. | salga, salgas, salga, salgamos, salgáis, salgan |
| Tú command | sal |

### ser-to be

| | |
|---|---|
| Present ind. | soy, eres, es, somos, sois, son |
| Preterit | fui, fuiste, fue, fuimos, fuisteis, fueron |
| Imperfect ind. | era, eras, era, éramos, erais, eran |
| Present subj. | sea, seas, sea, seamos, seáis, sean |
| Imperfect subj. | fuera, fueras, fuera, fuéramos, fuerais, fueran |
| Tú command | sé |

### tener-to have

| | |
|---|---|
| Present ind. | tengo, tienes, tiene, tenemos, tenéis, tienen |
| Preterit | tuve, tuviste, tuvo, tuvimos, tuvisteis, tuvieron |
| Future | tendré, tendrás, tendrá, tendremos, tendréis, tendrán |
| Condtional | tendría, tendrías, tendría, tendríamos, tendríais, tendrían |
| Present subj. | tenga, tengas, tenga, tengamos, tengáis, tengan |
| Imperfect subj. | tuviera, tuvieras, tuviera, tuviéramos, tuvierais, tuvieran |
| Tú command | ten |

### traer-to bring

| | |
|---|---|
| Present ind. | traigo, traes, trae, traemos, traéis, traen |

| | |
|---|---|
| Preterit | traje, trajiste, trajo, trajimos, trajisteis, trajeron |
| Present subj. | traiga, traigas, traiga, traigamos, traigáis, traigan |
| Imperfect subj. | trajera, trajeras, trajera, trajéramos, trajerais, trajeron |
| Present part. | trayendo |
| Past part. | traído |

## venir-to come

| | |
|---|---|
| Present ind. | vengo, vienes, viene, venimos, venís, vienen |
| Preterit | vine, viniste, vino, vinimos, vinisteis, vinieron |
| Future | vendré, vendrás, vendrá, vendremos, vendréis, vendrán |
| Condtional | vendría, vendrías, vendría, vendríamos, vendríais, vendrían |
| Present subj. | venga, vengas, venga, vengamos, vengáis, vengan |
| Imperfect subj. | viniera, vinieras, viniera, viniéramos, vinierais, vinieran |
| Present part. | viniendo |
| Tú command | ven |

## ver-to see

| | |
|---|---|
| Present ind. | veo, ves, ve, vemos, veis, ven |
| Preterit | vi, viste, vio, vimos, visteis, vieron |
| Imperfect ind. | veía, veías, veía, veíamos, veíais, veían |
| Past part. | visto |

# *APPENDIX II*

# Verb List

**Spanish-English**

**A**

| | |
|---|---|
| abandonar | to abandon |
| abrazar | to hug |
| abrir | to open |
| aburrir | to bore |
| abusar | to abuse |
| acabar | to finish, end |
| aceptar | to accept |
| acercarse | to approach |
| acompañar | to accompany |
| aconsejar | to advise |
| acordarse | to remember |
| acostarse | to go to bed |
| acostumbrarse | to become accustomed |
| actuar | to act |
| admirar | to admire |
| admitir | to admit |
| advertir | to warn |
| afectar | to affect |
| afeitarse | to shave |
| agarrar | to grab |
| agradecer | to thank |
| ahogar | to drown |
| ahorrar | to save |
| almorzar | to eat lunch |
| alquilar | to rent |
| amar | to love (people) |
| andar | to go around |
| anunciar | to announce |
| apagar | to turn off |
| aparecer | to appear |
| apoyar | to support |
| apreciar | to appreciate |
| aprender | to learn |
| aprobar | to pass a test |
| apurarse | to hurry |
| arrancar | to start (car), pull up |
| arreglar | to fix, arrange |
| asegurar | to assure |
| asesinar | to murder |
| asistir | to attend (class) |
| asustar | to scare |
| atacar | to attack |
| atraverse | to dare |
| atropellar | to run over |
| aumentar | to increase |
| averiguar | to find out |
| ayudar | to help |

**B**

| | |
|---|---|
| bailar | to dance |
| bajar | to go/come down |
| bañar(se) | to bathe (oneself) |
| barrer | to sweep |
| beber | to drink |
| besar | to kiss |
| borrar | to erase |
| botar | to throw out |
| buscar | to look for |

**C**

| | |
|---|---|
| caerse | to fall |
| caber | to fit |
| calmar | to calm down |
| callarse | to be quiet |
| cambiar | to change |
| caminar | to walk |
| cansarse | to get tired |
| cantar | to sing |
| casarse | to get married |
| castigar | to punish |
| cazar | to hunt |
| celebrar | to celebrate |

| | | | |
|---|---|---|---|
| cenar | to eat supper/dinner | **D** | |
| cepillar | to brush | | |
| cerrar | to close | dar | to give |
| cocinar | to cook | deber | to owe, should, must |
| coger | to catch, seize | decidir | to decide |
| colgar | to hang | decir | to say, tell |
| comenzar | to commence, start, begin | declarar | to declare |
| comer | to eat | defender | to defend |
| cometer | to commit | dejar | to leave behind, allow |
| competir | to compete | demostrar | to demonstrate |
| comprar | to buy | depender | to depend |
| comprender | to understand | deprimir | to depress |
| conducir | to drive, conduct | desaparecer | to disappear |
| confiar | to trust | desayunar | to eat breakfast |
| conjugar | to conjugate | descansar | to rest |
| conocer | to know, be familiar with | descender | to descend |
| conseguir | to get, obtain | describir | to describe |
| consentir | to consent | descubrir | to discover |
| construir | to build | desear | to wish, desire |
| contar | to count | desmayarse | to faint |
| contener | to contain | despedir(se) | to fire (say goodbye) |
| contestar | to answer | despertarse | to wake up |
| continuar | to continue | despreciar | to look down on |
| contribuir | to contribute | destruir | to destroy |
| convencer | to convince | desvestir(se) | to undress (oneself) |
| conversar | to converse | detener | to detain |
| convertir | to convert | devolver | to return (something) |
| corregir | to correct | dibujar | to draw |
| correr | to run | dirigir | to direct |
| cortar | to cut | discutir | to discuss |
| costar | to cost | disminuir | to diminish |
| crear | to create | distinguir | to distinguish |
| crecer | to grow | distraer | to distract |
| creer | to believe | distribuir | to distribute |
| criar | to rear | divertirse | to enjoy, have a good time |
| criticar | to criticize | dividir | to divide |
| cruzar | to cross | doblar | to turn, fold |
| cubrir | to cover | doler | to hurt |
| cuidar | to take care of | dormir | to sleep |
| cumplir | to complete | ducharse | to (take a) shower |
| curar | to cure | dudar | to doubt |
| | | | |
| **CH** | | **E** | |
| charlar | to chat | | |
| chillar | to scream | echar | to throw, put |
| chismear | to gossip | ejecutar | to execute |
| chocar | to collide | elegir | to choose |

| | | | |
|---|---|---|---|
| eliminar | to eliminate | **G** | |
| empezar | to start, begin | | |
| enamorarse | to fall in love | ganar | to win, earn |
| encantar | to love (not people) | gastar | to spend (money) |
| encender | to light, turn on | girar | to rotate |
| encontrar(se) | to find, (meet) | golpear | to hit |
| enfermarse | to get sick | gozar | to enjoy |
| engañar | to deceive | graduarse | to graduate |
| enojarse | to become angry | gritar | to scream |
| enrojecer | to turn red | guardar | to guard, keep, put away |
| enseñar | to teach, show | guiar | to guide |
| ensuciar | to get dirty | gustar | to please, be pleasing to |
| entender | to understand | | |
| enterrar | to bury | | |
| entrar | to enter | **H** | |
| entregar | to turn in | | |
| entristecerse | to become sad | haber | to have, exist |
| envejecerse | to become old | hablar | to speak, talk |
| enviar | to send | hacer | to do, make |
| escaparse | to escape | hallar | to find |
| escoger | to choose | herir | to injure |
| esconder | to hide | huir | to flee |
| escribir | to write | | |
| escuchar | to listen to | | |
| esperar | to wait, hope | **I** | |
| esquiar | to ski | | |
| establecer | to establish | imaginarse | to imagine |
| estar | to be | impedir | to impede |
| estudiar | to study | imponer | to impose |
| evitar | to avoid | importar | to matter, be important |
| exagerar | to exaggerate | incluir | to include |
| examinar | to examine | indicar | to indicate |
| exigir | to demand | influir | to influence |
| existir | to exist | insistir | to insist |
| explicar | to explain | instruir | to instruct |
| extinguir | to extinguish | interesar | to interest |
| | | invertir | to invest |
| | | invitar | to invite |
| **F** | | ir(se) | to go (away) |
| faltar | to lack | irritar | to irritate |
| fascinar | to fascinate | | |
| fastidiar | to annoy | | |
| felicitar | to congratulate | **J** | |
| fingir | to pretend | | |
| firmar | to sign | | |
| fracasar | to fail | jubilarse | to retire |
| fumar | to smoke | jugar | to play (games, sports) |
| funcionar | to work, function | jurar | to swear |
| fusilar | to shoot | juzgar | to judge |

## L

| | |
|---|---|
| ladrar | to bark |
| lamentar | to be sorry about |
| lastimar | to hurt, injure |
| lavar | to wash |
| leer | to read |
| levantar(se) | to lift, raise (get up) |
| limpiar | to clean |
| lograr | to achieve |
| luchar | to fight |

## LL

| | |
|---|---|
| llamar(se) | to call, (be named) |
| llegar | to arrive |
| llenar | to fill, fill out |
| llevar | to take along, carry, wear |
| llorar | to cry |
| llover | to rain |

## M

| | |
|---|---|
| madurar | to mature, ripen |
| maltratar | to mistreat |
| mandar | to send, order |
| manejar | to drive |
| mantener | to maintain |
| maquillarse | to put on makeup |
| marcharse | to leave |
| matar | to kill |
| matricularse | to enroll, register |
| medir | to measure |
| mejorarse | to get better |
| mencionar | to mention |
| mentir | to lie |
| merecer | to deserve |
| meter | to insert, put in |
| mirar | to watch, look at |
| mojar | to moisten |
| molestar | to bother |
| montar | to ride |
| morder | to bite |
| morir | to die |
| mostrar | to show |
| mover | to move |
| mudarse | to move, relocate |
| pescar | to fish |
| pintar | to paint |
| planchar | to iron |

## N

| | |
|---|---|
| nacer | to be born |
| nadar | to swim |
| necesitar | to need |
| negar | to deny |
| nevar | to snow |

## O

| | |
|---|---|
| obligar | to force |
| observar | to observe |
| obtener | to get, obtain |
| ocupar | to occupy |
| ocurrir | to occur |
| odiar | to hate |
| ofender | to offend |
| ofrecer | to offer |
| oír | to hear |
| oler | to smell |
| olvidar | to forget |
| oponer | to oppose |
| orar | to pray |
| ordenar | to order, arrange |

## P

| | |
|---|---|
| pagar | to pay |
| pararse | to stop |
| parecer(se) | to seem, (look like) |
| participar | to participate |
| pasar | to pass, spend (time) |
| pasear | to take a walk |
| pedir | to ask for, request |
| pegar | to hit |
| peinar(se) | to comb (one's) hair |
| pelear | to fight |
| pensar | to think, plan |
| perder | to lose |
| perdonar | to excuse, pardon |
| permanecer | to stay, remain |
| permitir | to permit |
| perseguir | to pursue, chase |
| persistir | to persist |
| persuadir | to persuade |
| pertenecer | to belong |
| pesar | to weigh |
| regresar | to return |
| reír | to laugh |
| relajar | to relax |

| | | | |
|---|---|---|---|
| **plantar** | to plant | **repetir** | to repeat |
| **platicar** | to chat | **requerir** | to require |
| **poder** | to be able, can | **resolver** | to resolve |
| **poner** | to put, place | **respirar** | to breathe |
| **poner(se)** | to put on clothes, become | **responder** | to respond |
| **practicar** | to practice | **rezar** | to pray |
| **preferir** | to prefer | **robar** | to rob, steal |
| **preguntar** | to ask (a question) | **rogar** | to beg, plead |
| **prender** | to turn on | **romper** | to break, tear |
| **preocuparse** | to worry | | |
| **preparar** | to prepare | | |
| **prestar** | to lend | | |
| **probar(se)** | to taste, to try (on clothes) | | |
| **producir** | to produce | | |
| **prohibir** | to prohibit | | |
| **prometer** | to promise | | |
| **pronunciar** | to pronounce | | |
| **proteger** | to protect, guard | | |
| **protestar** | to protest | | |
| **proveer** | to provide | | |

## S

| | | | |
|---|---|---|---|
| | | **saber** | to know (facts, information) |
| | | **saltar** | to jump |
| | | **saludar** | to greet, say hello |
| | | **satisfacer** | to satisfy |
| | | **secar** | to dry |
| | | **seguir** | to follow, continue |
| | | **sentar(se)** | to seat, (sit down) |
| | | **sentir(se)** | to touch, (feel) |
| | | **ser** | to be |
| | | **servir** | to serve |
| | | **significar** | to mean, signify |
| | | **sobrevivir** | to survive |
| | | **solicitar** | to apply for |
| | | **soltar** | to let go |
| | | **sonar** | to sound, ring |
| | | **soñar** | to dream |
| | | **sonreír** | to smile |
| | | **soportar** | to put up with |
| | | **sorprender** | to surprise |
| | | **sostener** | to sustain |
| | | **subir** | to go up, get on |
| | | **suceder** | to happen |
| | | **sudar** | to sweat |
| | | **sufrir** | to suffer |
| | | **sugerir** | to suggest |
| | | **suponer** | to suppose |
| | | **suspirar** | to sigh |
| | | **sustituir** | to substitute |

## Q

| | |
|---|---|
| **quedarse** | to stay, remain |
| **quejarse** | to complain |
| **quemar** | to burn |
| **querer** | to want, love |
| **quitar** | to take away |
| **quitarse** | to take off clothes |

## R

| | |
|---|---|
| **realizar** | to achieve, accomplish |
| **recibir** | to receive |
| **recoger** | to pick up |
| **recomendar** | to recommend |
| **reconocer** | to recognize |
| **recordar** | to remember, remind |
| **rechazar** | to reject |
| **reducir** | to reduce |
| **referir** | to refer |
| **regalar** | to give as a gift |
| **regañar** | to gripe, scold |

## T

| | |
|---|---|
| **tardar** | to be late, delay |
| **temer** | to fear |
| **tener** | to have |
| **terminar** | to finish |
| **tirar** | to throw, pull |
| **tocar** | to play an instrument, knock |
| **tomar** | to drink, to take |
| **toser** | to cough |
| **trabajar** | to work |
| **traducir** | to translate |
| **traer** | to bring |
| **tragar** | to swallow |
| **tratar** | to try, treat |
| **tronar** | to thunder |

## U

| | |
|---|---|
| **unir** | to unite |
| **usar** | to use, wear |
| **utilizar** | to use, utilize |

## V

| | |
|---|---|
| **vaciar** | to empty |
| **valer** | to be worth |
| **vender** | to sell |
| **venir** | to come |
| **ver** | to see |
| **vestirse** | to dress (get dressed) |
| **viajar** | to travel |
| **visitar** | to visit |
| **vivir** | to live |
| **volar** | to fly |
| **volver** | to return |

# English-Spanish

## A

| | |
|---|---|
| to abandon | abandonar |
| to abuse | abusar |
| to accept | aceptar |
| to accompany | acompañar |
| to achieve | lograr |
| to achieve | realizar |
| to act | actuar |
| to admire | admirar |
| to admit | admitir |
| to advise | aconsejar |
| to affect | afectar |
| to announce | anunciar |
| to annoy | fastidiar |
| to answer | contestar |
| to appear | aparecer |
| to apply for | solicitar |
| to appreciate | apreciar |
| to approach | acercarse |
| to arrive | llegar |
| to ask a (question) | preguntar |
| to ask for, request | pedir |
| to assure | asegurar |
| to attack | atacar |
| to attend (class) | asistir |
| to avoid | evitar |

## B

| | |
|---|---|
| to bark | ladrar |
| to bathe | bañar |
| to be | estar |
| to be | ser |
| to be able, can | poder |
| to be born | nacer |
| to be late, delay | tardar |
| to be quiet | callarse |
| to be sorry about | lamentar |
| **to be worth** | **valer** |
| to become angry | enojarse |
| to become old | envejecerse |
| to call (be named) | llamar(se) |

## C

| | |
|---|---|
| to calm down | calmar |
| to catch, seize | coger |
| to celebrate | celebrar |
| to change | cambiar |
| to chat | charlar |
| to chat | platicar |
| to choose | escoger |
| to choose, select | elegir |
| to clean | limpiar |
| to close | cerrar |
| to collide | chocar |
| to comb | peinar |
| **to come** | **venir** |
| to start, begin | comenzar |
| to commit | cometer |
| to compete | competir |
| to complain | quejarse |
| to complete | cumplir |
| to congratulate | felicitar |
| to conjugate | conjugar |
| to consent | consentir |
| to contain | contener |
| to continue | continuar |
| to contribute | contribuir |
| to converse | conversar |
| to convert | convertir |
| to convince | convencer |
| to cook | cocinar |
| to correct | corregir |
| to cost | costar |
| to cough | toser |
| to count | contar |
| to cover | cubrir |
| to create | crear |
| to criticize | criticar |
| to cross | cruzar |
| to cry | llorar |
| to cure | curar |
| to cut | cortar |

## D

| | |
|---|---|
| to dance | **bailar** |
| to dare | **atraverse** |
| to deceive | **engañar** |
| to decide | **decidir** |
| to declare | **declarar** |
| to defend | **defender** |
| to demand | **exigir** |
| to demonstrate | **demostrar** |
| to deny | **negar** |
| to depend | **depender** |
| to depress | **deprimir** |
| to descend | **descender** |
| to describe | **describir** |
| to deserve | **merecer** |
| to destroy | **destruir** |
| to detain | **detener** |
| to die | **morir** |
| to diminish | **disminuir** |
| to direct | **dirigir** |
| to disappear | **desaparecer** |
| to discover | **descubrir** |
| to discuss | **discutir** |
| to distinguish | **distinguir** |
| to distract | **distraer** |
| to distribute | **distribuir** |
| to divide | **dividir** |
| to do, make | **hacer** |
| to doubt | **dudar** |
| to draw | **dibujar** |
| to dream | **soñar** |
| **to get dressed** | **vestirse** |
| to drink | **beber** |
| to drink, to take | **tomar** |
| to drive | **manejar** |
| to drive, conduct | **conducir** |
| to drown | **ahogar** |
| to dry | **secar** |

## E

| | |
|---|---|
| to eat | **comer** |
| to eat breakfast | **desayunar** |
| to eat lunch | **almorzar** |
| to eat supper/dinner | **cenar** |
| to eliminate | **eliminar** |
| **to empty** | **vaciar** |
| to enjoy | **gozar** |
| to enroll, register | **matricularse** |
| to enter | **entrar** |
| to erase | **borrar** |
| to escape | **escaparse** |
| to establish | **establecer** |
| to exaggerate | **exagerar** |
| to examine | **examinar** |
| to excuse, pardon | **perdonar** |
| to execute | **ejecutar** |
| to exist | **existir** |
| to explain | **explicar** |
| to extinguish | **extinguir** |

## F

| | |
|---|---|
| to fail | **fracasar** |
| to faint | **desmayar** |
| to fall | **caerse** |
| to fall in love | **enamorarse** |
| to fascinate | **fascinar** |
| to fear | **temer** |
| to feel | **sentirse** |
| to fight | **luchar** |
| to fight | **pelear** |
| to fill, fill out | **llenar** |
| to find, (meet up) | **encontrar(se)** |
| to find | **hallar** |
| to find out | **averiguarse** |
| to finish | **terminar** |
| to finish, end | **acabar** |
| to fish | **pescar** |
| to fit | **caber** |
| to fix, arrange | **arreglar** |
| to flee | **huir** |
| **to fly** | **volar** |
| to follow, continue | **seguir** |
| to force | **obligar** |
| to forget | **olvidar** |

## G

| | |
|---|---|
| to get better | **mejorarse** |
| to get dirty | **ensuciar** |
| to get married | **casarse** |
| to get sick | **enfermarse** |
| to get tired | **cansarse** |
| to get, obtain | **conseguir** |
| to get, obtain | **obtener** |
| to give | **dar** |
| to give as a gift | **regalar** |
| to go | **ir** |

| | | | |
|---|---|---|---|
| to go away | irse | to invite | invitar |
| to go around | andar | to iron | planchar |
| to go to bed | acostarse | to irritate | irritar |
| to go up, get on | subir | | |
| to go/come down | bajar | | |
| to gossip | chismear | **J** | |
| to grab | agarrar | | |
| to graduate | graduarse | to judge | juzgar |
| to greet, say hello | saludar | to jump | saltar |
| to gripe, scold | regañar | | |
| to grow | crecer | **K** | |
| to guard, keep | guardar | | |
| to guide | guiar | to kill | matar |
| | | to kiss | besar |
| | | to know, be familiar | conocer |
| **H** | | | |
| | | **L** | |
| to hang | colgar | | |
| to happen | suceder | to lack | faltar |
| to hate | odiar | to laugh | reír |
| to have | tener | to learn | aprender |
| to enjoy oneself | divertirse | to leave | marcharse |
| **to have, exist** | **haber** | to leave behind | dejar |
| to hear | oír | to lend | prestar |
| to help | ayudar | to let go | soltar |
| to hide | esconder | to lie | mentir |
| to hit | golpear | to get up | levantarse |
| to hit | pegar | to lift, raise | levantar |
| to hug | abrazar | to light, turn on | encender |
| to hunt | cazar | to listen to | escuchar |
| to hurry | apurarse | **to live** | **vivir** |
| to hurt | doler | to look down on | despreciar |
| to hurt, injure | lastimar | to look for | buscar |
| | | to lose | perder |
| | | to love (not people) | encantar |
| **I** | | to love (people) | amar |
| to imagine | imaginarse | | |
| to impede | impedir | **M** | |
| to impose | imponer | | |
| to include | incluir | to matter | importar |
| to increase | aumentar | to mature, ripen | madurar |
| to indicate | indicar | to mean, signify | significar |
| to influence | influir | to measure | medir |
| to injure | herir | to mention | mencionar |
| to insert, put in | meter | to mistreat | maltratar |
| to insist | insistir | to moisten | mojar |
| to instruct | instruir | to move | mover |
| to interest | interesar | | |
| to invest | invertir | | |

| | | | |
|---|---|---|---|
| to move, relocate | **mudarse** | to punish | **castigar** |
| to murder | **asesinar** | to pursue, chase | **perseguir** |
| | | to put, place | **poner** |
| | | to put on clothes | **ponerse** |
| **N** | | to put on make up | **maquillarse** |
| | | to put up with | **soportar** |
| to need | **necesitar** | | |
| | | **R** | |
| **O** | | | |
| | | to rain | **llover** |
| to observe | **observar** | to read | **leer** |
| to occupy | **ocupar** | to rear | **criar** |
| to occur | **ocurrir** | to receive | **recibir** |
| to offend | **ofender** | to recognize | **reconocer** |
| to offer | **ofrecer** | to recommend | **recomendar** |
| to open | **abrir** | to reduce | **reducir** |
| to oppose | **oponer** | to refer | **referir** |
| to order, arrange | **ordenar** | to reject | **rechazar** |
| to owe, should, must | **deber** | to relax | **relajar** |
| | | to remember | **acordarse** |
| | | to remember | **recordar** |
| **P** | | to rent | **alquilar** |
| | | to repeat | **repetir** |
| to paint | **pintar** | to require | **requerir** |
| to participate | **participar** | to resolve | **resolver** |
| to pass a test | **aprobar** | to respond | **responder** |
| to pass, spend (time) | **pasar** | to rest | **descansar** |
| to pay | **pagar** | to retire | **jubilarse** |
| to permit | **permitir** | to return | **regresar** |
| to persist | **persistir** | to return | **volver** |
| to persuade | **persuadir** | to return (something) | **devolver** |
| to pick up | **recoger** | to ride | **montar** |
| to plant | **plantar** | to rob, steal | **robar** |
| to play an instrument | **tocar** | to rotate | **girar** |
| to play (games, sports) | **jugar** | to run | **correr** |
| to please | **gustar** | to run over | **atropellar** |
| to practice | **practicar** | | |
| to pray | **orar** | | |
| to pray | **rezar** | **S** | |
| to prefer | **preferir** | | |
| to prepare | **preparar** | to satisfy | **satisfacer** |
| to pretend | **fingir** | to save | **ahorrar** |
| to produce | **producir** | to fire, dismiss | **despedir** |
| to prohibit | **prohibir** | to say goodbye | **despedirse** |
| to promise | **prometer** | to say, tell | **decir** |
| to pronounce | **pronunciar** | to scare | **asustar** |
| to protect | **proteger** | to scream | **chillar** |
| to protest | **protestar** | to scream, | **gritar** |
| to provide | **proveer** | to sit down | **sentarse** |

| | | | |
|---|---|---|---|
| to see | ver | to think, plan | pensar |
| to seem (look like) | parecer(se) | to throw out | botar |
| **to sell** | **vender** | to throw, pull | tirar |
| to send | enviar | to throw, put | echar |
| to send, order | mandar | to thunder | tronar |
| to serve | servir | to touch, knock | tocar |
| to shave | afeitarse | to translate | traducir |
| to shoot | fusilar | **to travel** | **viajar** |
| to show | mostrar | to trust | confiar |
| to sigh | suspirar | to try, taste | probar |
| to sign | firmar | to try on clothes | probarse |
| to sing | cantar | to try, treat | tratar |
| to ski | esquiar | to turn in | entregar |
| to sleep | dormir | to turn off | apagar |
| to smell | oler | to turn on | prender |
| to smile | sonreír | to turn red | enrojecer |
| to smoke | fumar | to turn, fold | doblar |
| to snow | nevar | | |
| to sound, ring | sonar | | |
| to speak, talk | hablar | **U** | |
| to spend (money) | gastar | | |
| to start a car | arrancar | to understand | comprender |
| to start, begin | empezar | to understand | entender |
| to stay, remain | permanecer | to undress | desvestirse |
| to stay, remain | quedarse | **to unite** | **unir** |
| to stop | pararse | **to use, utilize** | **utilizar** |
| to study | estudiar | to use, wear | usar |
| to substitute | sustituir | | |
| to suffer | sufrir | | |
| to suggest | sugerir | **V** | |
| to support | apoyar | | |
| to suppose | suponer | to visit | visitar |
| to surprise | sorprender | | |
| to survive | sobrevivir | | |
| to sustain | sostener | **W** | |
| to swallow | tragar | | |
| to swear | jurar | to wait, hope | esperar |
| to sweat | sudar | to wake up | despertarse |
| to sweep | barrer | to walk | caminar |
| to swim | nadar | to want, love | querer |
| | | to warn | advertir |
| | | to wash | lavar |
| **T** | | to watch, look at | mirar |
| | | to weigh | pesar |
| to take a walk | pasear | to win, earn | ganar |
| to take away | quitar | to wish, desire | desear |
| to take care of | cuidar | to work | trabajar |
| to take off clothes | quitarse | to work, function | funcionar |
| to teach, show | enseñar | to worry | preocupar |
| to thank | agradecer | to write | escribir |

# REFERENCES

Ayllón, Candido, Paul Smith, and Antonio Morillo. 1992. *Spanish composition through literature.* Englewood Cliffs: Prentice Hall.

Brown, Roger and Albert Gilman. 1960. The pronouns of power and solidarity. In *Style in language,* ed. T.A. Sebeok, 253-76. Cambridge, Mass: MIT Press.

Bull, William. 1965. *Spanish for teachers: Applied linguistics.* New York: Ronald Press.

Butt, John and Carmen Benjamin. 1988. *A new reference grammar of modern Spanish.* London: Edward Arnold.

Chastain, Kenneth. 1980. Native speaker reaction to instructor-identified student second language errors. *Modern Language Journal* 64: 210-215.

Ellis, Rod. 1985. *Understanding second language acquisition.* Oxford: Oxford University Press.

Ensz, Kathleen. 1982. A study of the use and acceptability of target-language communication strategies employed by American students of Russian. *Modern Language Journal* 66: 133-39.

Good, C. Edward. 2002. *Whose grammar book is this anyway?* New York: MJF Books.

Iglesias, Mario and Walter Meiden. 1995. *Spanish for oral and written review.* Fort Worth: Harcourt Brace College Publishers.

Lightblown, Patsy and Nina Spada. 1990. Focus on form and corrective feedback in communicative language teaching: Effects of second language learning. *Studies in second language acquisition* 12: 429-48.

Ludwig, Jeanette. 1984. Native speaker judgments of second language learners' efforts at communication: A review. *Modern Language Journal* 66: 274-83.

Myhill, Debra. 2000. Misconceptions and difficulties in the acquisition of metalinguistic knowledge. *Language and education* 14: 151-163.

Piazza, Linda. 1980. French tolerance of grammatical errors made by Americans. *Modern Language Journal* 64: 422-27.

Pountain, Christopher. 2003. *Exploring the Spanish language.* London: Hodder Arnold.

Schwenter, Scott. 1993. Diferencia dialectal por medio de pronombres: Una comparación del uso de tú y usted en España y México. Nueva Revista de Filología Hispánica 41:127-49.

Solé, Yolanda and Carlos Solé. 1977. *Modern Spanish grammar: A study in contrast.* Lexington: D. C. Heath and Company.

Tarone, Elaine. 1983. On the variability of interlanguage systems. *Applied Linguistics* 4:142-63.

Whitley, Stanley. 1986. *Spanish/English contrasts.* Washington D. C.: Georgetown University Press.

# INDEX

a causa de, 85
adjectives
    apocopation, 102
    demonstrative, 64
    formation, 101
    limiting, 108
    meaning-change, 106
    position of, 103
    possessive, 108
adverbs
    formation, 147
**alegre**, 110
commands
    **nosotros**, 140
    position of pronouns, 141
    **tú**, 139
    **usted/ustedes**, 138
    **vosotros**, 140
**como**, 86
conditional perfect tense, 28
conditional tense, 27
    with probability, 27
conjunctions
    use of, 159
**conocer**, 69
**contento**, 110
**¿cuál?**, 49
    versus **¿qué?**, 49
definite article
    uses of, 39
    with generic reference, 42
**dejar**, 32
demonstrative pronouns, 64
direct object pronouns, 58
    position of, 59
**época**, 86
**estar**
    uses of, 91
    with adjectives, 92
    with resultant condition, 96
**feliz**, 110
future perfect tense, 26
future tense
    irregular stems, 24
    regular conjugations, 24
gerunds, 166
    *by* + gerund, 167
    *while* + gerund, 167
**gustar**, 169
**hacer una pregunta**, 99
**hacerse**, 143
**hora**, 86
imperfect indicative
    irregular verbs, 78

    regular conjugations, 78
    versus preterit, 79
    with states or conditions, 81
imperfect progressive, 20
indefinite articles, 46
indirect object pronouns, 58
infinitives
    after adjectives, 165
    after **al**, 165
    after prepositions, 164
    as nouns, 167
interlanguage, 8
**ir**, 32
**irse**, 32
**laísmo**, 63
**leísmo**, 63
**llegar a ser**, 144
**llevar**, 135
**loísmo**, 63
nominalization
    with definite articles, 44
    with **lo** and **lo que**, 45
nouns
    gender, 36
    number, 35
**para**
    versus **por**, 156
passive voice, 96
past participle
    irregular forms, 22
past perfect indicative
    regular conjugations, 23
**pedir**, 98
**pero**, 127
**poder**, 69
**ponerse**, 125, 143
**por**, 85, 157
    versus **para**, 156
**porque**, 85
**preguntar**, 98
prepositional pronouns, 55

prepositions, 148
    compound, 148
    **por** and **para**, 157
    simple, 148
prescriptivism
    versus descriptivism, 8
present indicative
    irregular verbs, 14
    regular conjugations, 11
    spelling-change verbs, 12
    stem-changing verbs, 13
    use of, 15

present perfect indicative
   regular conjugations, 21
   uses of, 22
present progressive
   regular conjugations, 19
   use of, 19
preterit tense
   irregular stem verbs, 75
   irregular verbs, 76
   regular conjugations, 73
   spelling-change verbs, 73
   stem-changing verbs, 75
   versus imperfect, 79
pronouns
   double object pronouns, 61
   formal and informal forms, 54
   position of object pronouns, 59
   redundant, 60
¿qué?, 49
   versus ¿cuál?, 49
**quitar**, 135
reflexive pronouns, 66
reverse constructions, 175
**saber**, 69
**sacar**, 135
**salir**, 32
**ser**
   uses of, 90
   with adjectives, 92
**sino**, 127
subject pronouns, 53
   uses of, 54
subjunctive
   imposition of will, 119
   in concessive sentences, 137
   in independent clauses, 137
   in noun clauses, 119
   past perfect, 117
   present, 113
   present perfect, 116
   sequence of tenses, 123
   versus indicative, 118
   with "if clauses", 133
   with adjective clauses, 129
   with adverbial clauses, 130
   with doubt, disbelief, denial, 120
   with emotional reaction, 120
   with impersonal expressions, 121
   with **ojalá que**, 122
**tiempo**, 86
*to become*, 143
**tomar**, 135
**venir**, 32
**volverse**, 144

www.ingramcontent.com/pod-product-compliance
Lightning Source LLC
Chambersburg PA
CBHW060512300426
44112CB00017B/2641